# THE VALLEY AND THE FARM

*Also by Monica Edwards*

THE UNSOUGHT FARM

THE CATS OF PUNCHBOWL FARM

THE BADGERS OF PUNCHBOWL FARM

Monica Edwards

# THE VALLEY AND THE FARM

*London*
Michael Joseph

First published in Great Britain by
MICHAEL JOSEPH LTD
52 Bedford Square
London W.C.1
1971



7181 0839 6

Printed in Great Britain by
Tonbridge Printers Ltd, in ten on twelve point Plantin
on paper supplied by P. F. Bingham Ltd
and bound by James Burn at Esher, Surrey

FOR

GOLDIE AND NATALKA AND NICHOLAS

'Now that my barn is burned down
I have a clearer view of the rising moon.'
(Old Chinese: told to me by Nicholas)

# ILLUSTRATIONS

# CHAPTER ONE

HULA is a devious cat. I say this knowing the temptation to endow one's animals with characters, so that sometimes one pauses to wonder how much is invented and how much really is their own.

Old Force, in contrast, was completely incapable of guile. All his sins – and they were many – he committed openly and honestly, with style.

I remember the summer of the broody hens. The coops, each with wire-netting run and population of fluffy chicks, appeared in the garden to the wonderment and fascination of the cats, who were continually to be found inspecting the matter.

Hula's approach was typical. Elegant and tiny, even for a Blue Burmese, her advance was subtle and inconspicuous. She would arrive at the nearest point to one of the coops and peer at it from jungles of azalea, daintily menacing. She would peer too towards the house and if she detected one of us she would flounce away, affecting to be on other business; but if not she would glide in to lurk behind the coop. From this hiding place she would make sorties, to the distraction of the resident hen who never knew when or where her sharp face would appear.

Old Force, a Siamese of great qualities, would swing off down the garden and notice the broody hens as one who had forgotten their existence. He would then make an immediate change of direction straight to the nearest coop and sit down with his usual heavy bump close to the netting. Here with completely plain intention he would turn his gaze on to the inhabitants. Now and again he would poke a paw through the mesh or chitter, his whiskers twitching, our presence making no difference. He was always shouted at if seen, and would walk off with great dignity, offence bristling out of him. Our feelings were naturally with the haunted hens, but one couldn't help admiring the effrontery of this honest cat.

That summer Amanda was staying with us. We have known her nearly all her life and I have written before of her camping years here. A student nurse now, she was spending her holidays at the farm, and that meant doing anything from dish-washing to milking or tractor-driving. It was the way she liked it, and wonderful for my husband Bill and me. She it was who chose with me the extra dozen of day-old chicks to make up the numbers our two hens could rear.

I had intended to get as usual Cuckoo Marans, which lay the darkest brown eggs of all; but we were too beguiled by the varieties offered and bought White Marans, Golden Welsummers, Black Minorcas and, 'What are those beautiful little hens with rosy breasts and dove-coloured wings?' we asked; we had never seen anything like them. 'Cream Legbars,' we were told. 'They lay green eggs, too.' The farmer showed us a sample and it was true. The chicks which I would have bought anyway for their exquisite plumage were going to give us a bonus of leaf-green eggs. Could one care about mere productivity from a flock such as these?

There were times when, between Force and Hula, we wondered if we would succeed in rearing the little flock but all survived, except for one white maran which wilted, as chicks do, and died in my cupped hands in the farmhouse kitchen. Only Hula's mate, the Brown Burmese Pardos, who I am sure is a natural Buddhist, sat and watched the chicks with amber eyes full of wonder and no carnal intentions. Too soon the chicks were past the fluffy stage and into a leggy adolescence, and Amanda and I were turning our care and anxiety towards another infant creature.

'Checkmate's calved,' Bill said when he came in to breakfast. 'It's a heifer-calf, premature, and about the smallest we've ever had.'

Checkmate was one of the best cows in our Jersey herd. When Amanda and I had admired her tiny calf we gave our minds to thinking of a name for it. In dairy herds each calf is usually given a name which indicates its family line. Our herd had several lines; there was for instance the Tree family founded by Maidenhair and including Ginkgo, Sequoia, Redwood, Quince and Spruce; and the Sea family founded by Seawitch and now including Dolphin, Starfish, Spindrift, Mermaid – called by a small grandchild Mermalade. Some families were difficult to name; the Shakespeare family was one of these – no one knows better than I do how few female characters Shakespeare used; we soon exhausted all the easy ones and came to Dark Lady. The Checker line was the most difficult of all; you can't call a cow Bishop or Pawn or even Knight. We already had Chessa and Checker and Checkmate herself. Amada finally came up with Trellis. 'It is at least checkered and it sounds nice.' So Trellis it was.

That afternoon Checkmate went down to milk fever, although Bill had given her the usual protective injection against it. She rallied after a second injection but before nightfall she had died. This is a grievous thing in a smallish herd where every animal is known individually and probably – like its dam and granddam – has been born and bred on one's farm. For visitors one of the sights of the farm was watching Bill call in the cows one by one as he wanted them for milking. From the whole herd gathered in the yard members would detach themselves as their names were called and weave through the others to their places in the milking parlour. All their characteristics were known to us – there was the one who gargled when she mooed, the one that leaned against walls, the one the children could ride, and so on. Losing one was losing a member of the clan.

There was of course also the financial aspect. Checkmate's value then was about £100. Her casualty carcass value was £5.

There was no good in thinking about these things. The immediate problem was the calf. Newborn calves need colostrum, the first-milk after birth. We had no other freshly calved cow to supply the need and it is difficult to rear a calf – especially a delicate calf – without it: there are substitutes but no really good one has yet been devised. It might be better not to try, Bill said; even if we succeeded the calf would probably never be a strong and useful member of the herd. Amanda and I looked at each other and knew at once that we were going to try.

Our neighbour farmers were interested but not one had just then a freshly calved cow. The need was urgent: we looked up my recipe for colostrum substitute and made up a jugful which we gave to the tiny Trellis in a baby's bottle. Amanda rubbed her all over to stir the blood circulation as Checkmate's rough licking would have done; we encouraged her to stand and move a little, but without our help she folded down into the straw, and presently we left her there snugged for the night.

Early in the morning as the cows came from the fields for milking,

Amanda went down to attend to her patient in the calf-box. The news when she came in was not good. The substitute feed was passing through undigested and Trellis was not interested in taking any more. She was shivering in the cool of the early morning and less able to stand alone even than the night before. At breakfast Bill was careful not to say he had told us so. Trying not to show that we thought he might have been right we decided to bring the calf into the kitchen. While Amanda collected sacks and straw I began on the telephone a wider hunt for colostrum.

Eventually I found, on the far side of Hindhead, a farmer with a newly calved cow. She had, he said, enough to spare, and since it could not be added to his bulk-milk we could have it for the collecting. This was wonderful news. With our hopes lifting we made up the emergency ward bed. This was beside the Aga in the inglenook where the cat basket usually was. The cats looked on in disapprobation while we moved their basket to a new territory and laid down in its place a foundation of paper sacks, on which straw and hessian made a comfortable bed.

Bill softened towards us and carried Trellis up from the calf-box. She looked almost hopelessly tiny and frail, her head drooped over his arms in the kitchen doorway. She was in the Jersey tradition a pale apricot colour with black muzzle and tail-flash. Long black lashes hung over dark half-closed eyes. It would be better, said the practical farmer, to shoot her now and save her the misery and us the time and effort, but there was no real conviction in his voice; he knew us both too well and is himself a softer-hearted man than he cares to admit. Naturally we took no notice and bent to arrange the fawn-like legs more comfortably as Bill lowered the orphan into her corner.

The cats peered at her from the top of the Aga and through our legs and round the chimney-corner, their eyes wide and black. Cattle they knew, but not cattle in the kitchen and certainly not in the rightful place for cats only.

The first of the twice daily colostrum lifts was run in high hope, Amanda holding steady the screw-top jar of orange milk as I drove along the rough short cut through beech woods. We were gone for less than an hour but the little calf was too frail when we returned to suck properly from the bottle.

'You ought to know, Nurse,' I said. 'What now?'

Glancing in, Bill once more did not tell us that he had told us so.

'Have we any brandy?' Amanda asked. 'It might make her strong enough to suckle.'

I went to check our alcoholic store. 'Only some rather splendid Benedictine; it was a Christmas present. We haven't opened it; brandy isn't one of our drinks.' I had the bottle in my hand.

'You aren't going to use that, are you? Cooking brandy would be half the price.'

I looked at it. 'It might easily be cheaper to use the best when we have it, rather than go out to buy some cheap stuff especially? And we have to think of time.'

'A little Complan?' Nurse suggested. 'There's some left over from the 'flu.'

'This is probably the only calf in the world,' I said as we spooned the mixture down Trellis's throat, 'to be reared on Benedictine and Complan.'

'You haven't reared her yet,' said Bill.

# CHAPTER TWO

FOR three days and nights Amanda and I geared ourselves and the household to premature baby care. We shared the mucking-out of the inglenook – 'It's what you get when you keep cows in the kitchen,' Amanda said, rushing out with an odorous sack – and the washing of the patient where necessary and the night shifts which the frequent small feeds involved.

The heap of comfortable cats lying against the Aga would regard us with owlish wonderment at these night sessions; but they were becoming used to the calf in the kitchen and all the fuss we made of her. They were asleep again before the feed was finished, their sides rising and falling softly, a tide of fur.

It was June, and suddenly all summer broke out in blue and gold and hotness. Only the dawns were cool and drenched with dew. Sleepily gazing out of the window after the early morning calf-feed, I could see the dark pathways the cows had made through the silver grass of Barn field as they had come down for the milking. There would be birds singing – fewer now than when we had first come to the farm – a cuckoo with his midsummer broken voice, woodpigeons so drowsily crooning that I felt the long yawn rising as I turned for the last two hours of sleep.

Very slowly the tiny calf began to improve. Our dashes for colostrum were made with higher hearts now we knew that she would take it without the usual patient persuasion. Maybe she would even struggle to her miniature black hoofs without our help. There came the day when she waggled her tail as suckling calves and lambs do when they are not too weak to try, and we knew that – barring new disaster – she was going to live.

Amanda made her a little halter and lead of coloured plaited string. When Trellis was strong enough we put it on her and led her out into the garden, tottering beside us. For a longer time each day she was tethered on the lawn in dappled sunshine, and strength grew in her. For us, tidying the lawn with a trowel was easier than mucking-out the inglenook: feeds were larger and fewer, and nights unbroken; there was time for other things. Amanda discharged the invalid from our Intensive Care Ward and put down a bed of deep straw for her in the calf-shed annexe: then she took a look out into the incredibly still blue-and-golden world and saw that Bill was cutting grass for silage. I looked over her shoulder and felt at once the familiar almost magnetic pull of fields and woods.

Amanda and I have always been willing – one might say eager – to drop everything and leave the house to look after itself when the urge to be out comes over us; and it comes fairly often. As some in moments of need reach out for a drink or cigarette I reach for wild places. Our cats are of like mind. Whenever I take down the shabby farm jacket from behind the back door, whether to garden, feed chickens or make for the woods, cats with the roving instinct will have noticed and come padding to join me. A nice lot we are to look after a hungry farmer and the houseful of friends and helpers we invariably seem to gather.

No cats were indoors on this June morning, but the smell of mown grass had come in. There was also of course the ubiquitous smell of cowdung – Farmers' Gold, so says Bill – all perfectly in keeping with an ancient farm. Old Force was immediately revealed wiggling a paw through the teenage chickens' netting; he looked up at me and said words to the effect that he was coming too. Hula now materialised obliquely from the rhododendrons, walking very delicately and prettily. She said nothing but came trotting, like a small silver fairy. A golden eye opened in the shade of a golden hypericum as we passed: it closed again as Pardos implied that home was heaven and a cat could have too much of the roving life and adventure. He had been liable to waves of homeliness since the year when he had been lost and outcast for nine cold wet weeks.

I was going out to the Wild Valley to look at the badger setts. It was my most usual walk and Hula and Forsyte knew this, forging on ahead through – to them – breast-high grass. The roar of the tractor zoomed up Barn field, a house-depth below in its different valley, and I looked down and saw Amanda driving it. One of the few who look their best in a bikini she was wearing a yellow one and she looked all gold, fair hair over golden skin. The orange forage-harvester she was towing blew from its arched neck and head a mane of mowings; it reminded me of a stallion, high and crested; two manes flying, the yellow and the green. I could hear a song tangled somewhere in the roar as I waved and turned away to my own valley.

The cats went rollicking ahead leaping like dolphins in the grass sea, and I followed thinking of tractors; the usefulness of them, the danger, the noise and the stink, the frustrations in coming to terms with them as – to me – with all machinery. I thought of my years of driving them until I could stand no more being deaf to birds singing and wind in the trees as well as numb to the scent of grass; I thought of the two tractors that ran away and the one that turned over, breaking Bill's arm; the one that crushed his ribs in the silo-barn.

I knew all about how horses can plough only an acre a day when a tractor can plough four, but still unreasonably I hankered after the horse days – the days, even, when there was no machinery at all: unreasonably because, if we had been farming in the old way there would have been no time for going out to the Wild Valley as I was going now.

I feel sad that so few now can have their wild place. People need this peace of aloneness so much more now, in the crowd and uproar of our times, but the wild places are going. Our species proliferates, spilling out of its towns and cities; more towns are called for and the forests and green fields are destroyed to make room for them. Must the forests always go? I wish this need not happen; that we could live underground like Hobbits or up in the air or under the sea, until we check finally our awful fecundity. If there is anything I can do to protect it, I know one place that will never go under concrete.

Now in June the Valley came to meet me, overflowing with a scent of honeysuckle which rose like a summer tide up the slopes of the fields that fall to the Valley woods. Floating on it came the sleepy call of woodpigeons – 'Tak two-oo coo-oos, Taffy' – which has all summer in it.

The gate into the Valley stood open for the cows to go down to the stream: just beside it a tall foxglove leaned, its tip curled like a shepherd's crook; a finger beckoning me. I didn't need any beckoning; but still I liked to stand for a minute and stare and listen and breathe in the scented air. I did not know how long I might have it.

The way to the Wild Valley

Hula, elegant and tiny

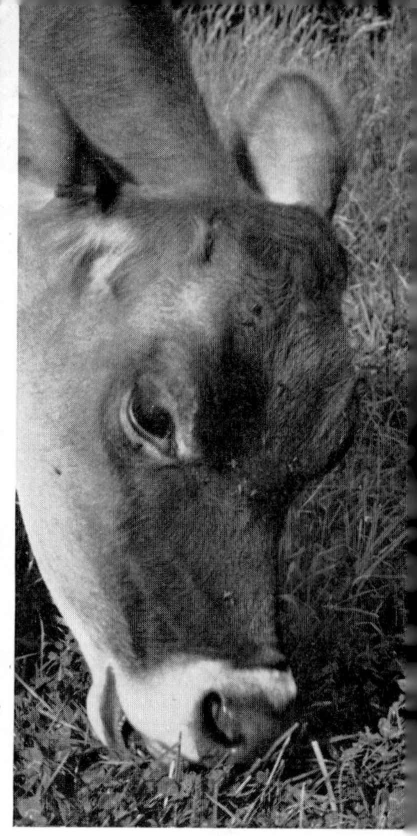

Amanda would bring Trellis up from the calf-shed

Trellis grown up

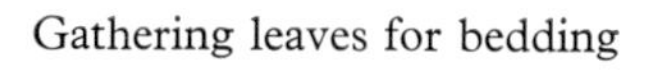

Gathering leaves for bedding

The Valley I hope will always be there, but I shall not. 'So few shopping days to Christmas,' a friend recently said to me, 'and by Christmas I mean death.' We were talking about music, and how little time there is to hear it all; he had spent a whole night playing records of Sibelius symphonies. He is thirty years old: how I envy him his shopping days! All the same, I know that this is silly, for how do we know what there is for us after death?

[illegible]ad gone on ahead of me, rollicking into the Valley, but [illegible] plaintive mew at the top of the steep field, Lower [illegible]os, my cissy Gingerbread Boy, who had changed [illegible] hastening anxiously after us. Pardos is a com- [illegible] very mixed-up kid. Essentially gentle, even [illegible]tbreaks of violence and quite fantastic brink- [illegible]rning dragon-slayer. He came now whirling [illegible] feet, too fast to save himself, his tail going round like a helicopter's propeller; and at that very moment six roe deer leapt fluidly from the trees to cross the grassy dell in front of us. Four had gone into the further wood when I saw, to my complete disbelief, Pardos rushing through the grass to launch himself at the flying hoofs of the two deer following.

He was a little sheepish, I thought, when having routed his dragons he returned to me, swivelling his ears and gently waving his tail. I was glad for him when I noticed that Hula, his adored Hula, had seen all, her silver fur betraying her in the bracken. A prudent cat, knowledgeable in hunting matters, she had watched and waited; but at least she had seen her Quixote tilt at his windmills. Probably she would think no better of him for it, but I liked to imagine that she would. It was hard for him to live up to a warrior like Old Force.

Talking afterwards to my son Sean about it – he was home from College that week-end – I said that perhaps Pardos felt his reputation needed some redeeming after staying behind to idle in the shade; but Sean said he thought that from his level my cissy cat had seen only the twinkling hoofs and not their superstructure, and supposing them to be fleeting mice had swiped into them.

Down in the Valley the stream made its gamelin music below the badgers' rampart. Above it the sunlight glimmered through a ceiling of young leaves. Spires of foxgloves swayed in the summer air. This is my perfect place, where no work of man comes; all is as it must have been long years ago. Down in the Valley I slip back in time and feel as if I were in the morning of the world.

The cats raced in and out of the badger holes, with what I used to think terrifying rashness, before I knew how far into the hillside the badger galleries go. My interest as always was in the signs the badgers had left outside; tracks on excavated sand, a pile of bracken-bedding thrown out, a small conical hole made by a snout which has found a beetle or a grub – a snozzle-hole in our family.

Among the tracks there were no small ones. These were disappointing times for badger-watchers; for the second year running there were no cubs. Other naturalists were telling the same story; and Dr Ernest Neal wrote that work was being done on a theory of badger infertility resulting from pesticides absorbed by worms. Badgers are omnivorous but worms form the largest single item of their diet. We use no pesticides on this farm, but badgers roam far in a night's foraging. It is heartening to hear of restrictions at last on chemicals whose use can destroy a whole ecological balance.

Coming home through the high pines, where sometimes on summer nights I take my sleeping bag, the three cats raced each other round and round and up the trees, making circles round grazing cows and my strolling legs. Hula was usually in front, less powerful than the mighty Forsyte but more swift. A field's length further I was surprised on turning to see her far behind and coming slowly. Then I saw that she was limping and I went back to meet her. She was carrying one foreleg. I picked her up, examining it as I walked, but I could see no injury although clearly it pained her. Then in minutes I saw that it was swelling and the probability, almost certainty, was plain – Hula had been bitten by an adder. Now I really hurried; and now the seriousness of the situation came home to me.

Sean was out in the car. No one was in the house as I ran to the telephone. Then, disaster on disaster, no response except a harsh buzz came through the receiver, bang and shout as I would. Incredibly, the phone was out of order.

Hula's leg was now three times at least its normal size, and she was distressed as one could well imagine. I rushed up to the attic for the cat-basket and putting her inside ran with it down the long drive to Rock Cottage. My neighbour Mary would lend me her car . . .

The car was gone from the garage and Mary with it. Her housekeeper, looking from the window, said their phone was out of order, too; it was a party line. I ran on, panting up the steep hill towards the next farm, and turning the corner met our own car and Sean returning.

It seemed less than a minute before Hula and I were in the car and he had turned and we were streaking down the lane. I shut my eyes at the corners and held the basket and crooned reassuringly to Hula. A confidence-inspiring driver on normal runs, I now experienced the kind of driving Sean could call up in emergency. 'I didn't take any risks,' he said to me seeing my face as we pulled up at the vet's. 'I never do on the road, least of all with you as passenger.'

'Not even calculated risks?'

He took the basket. 'Ma, you're a case.'

Hula had two injections and Sean and I some much-needed reassurance from our good vet, Mr Craig. There were not many deaths from adder-bite, he told us, except where the heart was weak; and he admired her courage. Clearly in pain she was calm over her injections and the strangeness of the journey and the place and the things that were happening to her. She came home on my knee in the car; she had always disliked the basket. When I picked her up she purred just a little and pushed her head under my jacket.

# CHAPTER THREE

It was an anxious night. Several times I went down to Hula and stroked her and talked to her. She purred for me each time a little, but she would not let me touch the swollen leg, nor would she lick it herself. It stuck out, gross and shapeless – she has such beautiful legs, slender and sleek and graceful.

In the early hours I noticed that the swelling was going down, and from then the improvement was swift. By the evening of that day she was nearly her normal self, but she was quiet and still limping.

The following day all was as it had ever been, only more so. The natural exuberance of this tiny cat seemed suddenly intensified, as if making up for lost hours. With the door and two big windows open to the summer she chose a small top window for her entry, involving a tricky double jump which she could only have done out of devilry.

Hula is a skilled window climber, scaling fly-like the most improbable surfaces. A favourite way of discomposing visitors is her ascent of the kitchen west window which anyway has no top entry and apparently leads to nowhere. Admittedly it has leaded panes; her exploits, I imagine, would otherwise be quite impossible.

We are perhaps at farmhouse tea, which is proper in an old farmhouse kitchen, and the visitor is gazing through the window at the great triple yew tree which shelters the house (and holds its Guardian Spirit, if you would believe legend) and perhaps at a cloak of pink clematis that lies on the well-house roof, when suddenly a small silver cat leaps into view and pauses a second on the window sill. Then under the startled gaze of the visitor she makes her moth-like run up the window and – positively – vanishes like a bird upwards. We of course know – but the visitor does not – that there is an oak beam in the line of her travel and that Sean's window is open above it. Presently we hear a soft thud on the ceiling which is also Sean's bedroom floor, and know that she has landed. There will soon be more thumps and bangs and scuffles if someone doesn't quickly retrieve her, and confusion among Sean's botanical and photographic papers. One can, of course, leave his west window shut, but then Hula scales this also to slip under the overhanging eaves into the roof space, where she creates tumult among the birds.

Mr Forsyte was a very different cat. His power was of the earth; he was not a cat for heights. I was surprised one day to hear his raucous voice blasting down to me from some unlikely level and went out to see where he was. A dismayed but commanding howl drew my eyes; he was, improbably, on the house-roof, peering down at me over the eaves with his electronic squint. His ears lay out flat at right-angles as he bawled at me what sounded like a blend of summons and threat; something to the effect of, 'Come and get me down out of here N-O-W, or I'll clobber you!'

Naturally we quickly got the ladder. Sean went up in true fireman style and rescued a furious thankless cat. It is always easier to go up than down, and we could only suppose that Old Force had been pursuing a bird and did not realise how far he had climbed.

For all his blundering ways he was not a cat to get stuck very often, and when he did he was always both enraged and appealing. It would be unkind to call him greedy, but he loved food, and when he did get into trouble this was usually the cause. There was the incident of the empty cat-meat tin, put down with the cats' dinners for a final lick-out. Hula and Pardos were delicate exponents of this skill, but Forsyte overdid his zeal that day and got his head stuck. The outraged muffled howl he produced fetched me up from the cellar where I was looking for a last bottle of damson wine which I wishfully imagined we had still not broached. The awful sight of my splendid royal cat charging round the kitchen with a tin on his head projected me to the rescue. He was not grateful, of course, and no doubt the whole thing was my fault. I had overlooked the width of those jowls and the power in neck and shoulder.

Now that Hula was herself again she resumed with gusto the temporarily halted rat campaign. There has never been a ratter like Hula among all our cats. She would not eat them, but she brought them in always for inspection – hulking grown monsters – and left them for my use and benefit. In my turn I passed them on for the use and benefit of the favoured among my plants. Already that year there was a rat buried beside nearly every lily bulb and two beside each glorious auratum. The passion flower on the south wall had a large one, adjured though one is by the books to poverty-strike this genus if flowers rather than foliage are wanted. (My plant on its rat diet covers itself in bloom, I may add, right up to the frosts.) On most mornings I would tour the garden with a rat on a trowel, looking around to decide on whom I would bestow this favour – trying to remember, too, where I had previously made donations, for it is not very pleasant to exhume earlier offerings in this line.

The infant Trellis was gaining weight and strength, and Amanda would bring her up from the calf-shed to enjoy the sunshine in the sheltered garden. I used to take out my canvas chair and rocky card table (*foreign*, says the explanatory legend underneath it: I bought it at a village jumble), and there settle beside her to the inexpressible toil and discipline of writing. Quite often I would not be writing at all – thinking about it, I would grandly tell my family – but looking with admiring pleasure at the orphan calf, who had so justified my tease-provoking prescriptions of choice Benedictine, Complan, egg and Aga-side stabling. Looking, too, in envy at Amanda flying about in her bikini, busy at the things I would so much rather be doing than writing. Inevitably on such sunshiny mornings there would be a last-minute rush-round to conjure up lunch.

'Don't worry!' Amanda would say as I looked helplessly into the larder. 'In this house hasty meals are always the nicest.' And so it often was. No time for proper cooking; let's do oven-eggs with chives in the little brown dishes and have salad with them. No time for pudding; let's skim the cream and whip up a syllabub with a spoonful of the brandy Trellis didn't use; and there's cheese and fruit. And a bottle of apple wine. This is food that a Hilton could not rival.

I missed Amanda when her fortnight was up and she had returned to the care of others, more numerous and needy. Such is my character that always I seem to be missing people; so many have stayed here in this old farmhouse, and nearly all become somehow members of our family and are sadly missed accordingly.

I think about the long line of farm students I have looked after for Bill, and even – though he hotly denies the need for this – protected from his occasional exasperation. Like all of us they have had their many aspects; comical, endearing, aggravating, loyal, sometimes even truly selfless. I shall always remember Richard Ives in the winter when Bill twice broke his leg and was for weeks on crutches. A student's day ends at five p.m. but Bill has always elected to milk an hour later, on his own, so that the cows should have a twelve hour interval between milkings. For three months of that winter Richard voluntarily gave up his evenings and milked for Bill, with all but one week-end included: and there was no martyrdom about him; all was done cheerfully and as if it were the most natural thing for an eighteen-year-old boy to be working a fourteen hour day.

For the sheer joy of having him around, our Old Etonian Humphrey remains unequalled; from the day he arrived for interview, older than the average student, six feet five inches tall in city suit, with bowler and rolled umbrella, looking so improbable that Bill decided there must be more in him than showed on the surface. There was. On Bill's own rating he proved one of the best for downright hard – and often dirty – work. An aristocrat of the old school, heir to seven hotels, six farms, one of England's oldest stately houses and 2,000 acres, Humphrey never had a penny for daily usage. He travelled by public transport or when available the Bentley of an aunt. In times when this was less usual than now he went up to Harrods to have his hair styled, by appointment, calling in to see his Harley Street doctor – for he was a hypochondriac – and returning by train and country bus.

I would meet him at the bus stop, a mile and a half from the farm, usually with the bus fare in my pocket since I knew he seldom had it. Now and again the bus would be in before me, and I would see Humphrey and the conductor leaning out from the platform looking for me as I drove up and flourished my coin. 'Near thing,' he would say as having bailed him out I trotted small and short-legged beside his elevation to the car. 'Thought you'd never make it and I'd be taken on to Hindhead.'

We would call on the way home at The Three Horse Shoes, where Humphrey had an account, and drink companionably together by way of repayment, and I would hear about life at Eton, in the Guards, in Portugal where the hotels were, and in the stately home where the fuel bills came to one hundred pounds a week. I would hear, too, about the merchantman in whose galley he had toiled learning about cooking from the bottom upwards, in view of the hotels he was to inherit – as he was learning farming in view of the farms – and about life in the kitchens of the Dorchester where he had taken stage two in this initiation.

I can unreservedly recommend the Dorchester to any aspiring chef, if Humphrey was a sample of its kitchen graduates. His soups and soufflés linger in my memory like themes in a favoured symphony. He it was who taught me to make a delectable garlic onion soup, and a casserole of Rum Prunes with thick cream fit for a royal table: but cooking was not his only domestic skill; he could sew and darn beautifully and had mastered knitting but found it boring and useless. 'Why should I marry?' he once said to me. 'Everything they can do I can do better.'

Humphrey's health worried me at first, until I came to terms with it. He looked so tall and slender with huge brown eyes, long-lashed, in a pale tragic face, and now and again he would come rushing in saying, 'Oh, my God! My heart!' and collapse on his bed, requiring to be sat with and talked to. I fell for this, and registered all the appropriate anxiety, until one day he said with a sheepish grin, 'I know I'm a hypochondriac; there's nothing wrong with me, really!'

All the same, he remains the only man I have ever heard of who could crack three ribs running for a bus; and this I swear he gave as the cause of it. Bill, always very hearty in matters of injury and the cure thereof, wrapped him round in yards of heavy-duty sticky plaster and urged him to think no more about it. Gamely, Humphrey followed this hard counsel with only occasional mutterings and gasps; but there came the day when the plaster was ripe for removal. Humphrey assessed the situation through his open shirt-front and came up doubtful, but Bill swept his fears aside. 'Nothing to it, old chap! Just let me get a grip on the end; one yank and you'll twirl like a top and it'll be off before you know I've started.'

A loud shriek startled me as Humphrey left the room. I found him presently sitting under the lamp in what he was pleased to call the drawing-room, bare to the waist and with a razor-blade in hand. I said 'bare' but this is no description of Humphrey's hairy chest. With immense care and concentration he was snipping this pelt, strand by strand, from the plaster stuck upon it. I laughed so much that I think he was a little cross with me; but he forgave me, for he let me do his back, and when I had a birthday a day or so later I found in my place on the table a bottle of Scotch (he kept a cellar in his wardrobe) with a large candle stuck in the top flickering jollily.

Humphrey had three singing voices, all of them good. He had been the head chorister at Eton, but he insisted that anyone could do it; it was a matter of application and training. I remember my mystification the first time I heard these voices, down in the milking parlour (where the acoustics are excellent) singing the Responses – bass, tenor and treble. Whoever did he have down there? Bill, I knew, had only one voice with about two notes. They were all, of course, Humphrey, singing with himself. I have never heard anything like it. In our small and ancient village church he used so to paralyse the rest of the congregation – and that with only one of his voices – that the service seemed to be sung solo, I feeling conspicuous beside him and he complaining afterwards of how weak were the efforts of our choir and congregation, compared to what was usual at Eton.

Humphrey had a splendid classical guitar, insured for some hundreds of pounds, on which in the evenings he would play Bach and Lalo; this usually after a hot bath deep enough to chill all the radiators, and in a sumptuous red silk dressing-gown printed with black dragons.

His Sub Rosa cigarettes and quite fearful snuff came by post from Burlington Arcade. He never got used to our farmhouse tea and tray supper. After eggs and toast and salad and scones and stone-ground bread and plum cake at six, he would be seized about half-way through the evening by intolerable pangs of hunger, and would dash down to The Shoes where a stint behind the bar would earn him a decent square meal, and probably convince the customers that we starved our students up here in the lonely backwoods.

I do not know where Humphrey is now; he has passed like a comet from my homely orbit, but his memory warmly and laughably remains.

Other asteroids rise in my mind – not comets, perhaps, but they too have their place in my sky. There was the girl, Jackie, so beautiful and tough; Alan, who lived for falcons – 'I'm only farming so that I can turn sheep on to the hills and spend my days hawking.' – 'Alan,' Bill told him, 'nothing dies as quickly as a sheep if you take your eyes off it.'

With the build of a rugger forward he yet had nothing of Humphrey's vitality. 'I know I'm idle; at least I know it,' he would say, and stand gazing at birds while the life of the farm went past him. He used to try to interest Bill and me in landscape gardening our rolling pastures; he left us to take up landscape gardening, and left that to study medicine after, astonishingly, being accepted by a London teaching hospital (on his rugger record, Bill maintained). With us again in three months carrying a grip and a large contemporary painting he told me, 'They wasted my time! But perhaps I wasted theirs,' he added magnanimously; and after a while left us, with his green and purple painting under his arm, to my sorrow to reappear no more.

There was Ben, comfortable and kind, who looked like Pooh Bear and started me on a long affair with week-end prize crossword puzzles; the skier Fritz who was so handsome one could scarcely believe it, and who brought from his village in the Tyrol a black umbrella because he understood that Englishmen always carried one. Wolfgang thought our English bedding insufferable (so do I, now we have gone over to continental quilts): Matthias was almost totally silent, despite our efforts to teach him the language, until one day he came in with the momentous announcement, declaimed without hesitation, 'A wahsp has this moment bitten me!'

Michael, also from Germany, lived in perpetual amazement and I think disapproval of Edwards life, and I suppose that somehow during (perhaps because of?) his stay here we did seem to be more eccentric than usual, and that is saying much. 'In Chermany this could never heppen, exectly,' he would say, as my friend Pat and I took the wrong road and made a spot decision to go somewhere else, or I set off down to the Valley at dusk with a corked face, a red lantern and a Siamese cat at heel, or Bill went mowing with nothing on, a pair of slips hung on the gear-lever, 'in case anyone comes.'

Michael was a mocking-bird, echoing meticulously every farm noise. He would moo in answer whenever a cow mooed, and with fifty of them this was often; he would say 'Bang!' when a hammer dropped, 'Boom!' when the milking parlour door slammed, 'Miau!' in answer to the cats and 'Hoo-hoo-hoo!' to all the tawny owls. It happened every time.

There was John, up whose trouser-leg an escaped mouse of Hula's once ran, to circle his waist (he must have worn his trews looser than I wear mine). When with strange staring eyes he announced that the mouse was climbing his chest I urged him to catch it and let it loose in the garden; but he leapt up and shook himself and the mouse flew out, and Hula recaptured and killed and ate it at once.

Jill – of whom I have written before – had a curtain of shining black hair. At least, it looked black to me, but she maintained that the blackberry coat of her Angus bull-calf made it look rusty, and she took to dying her own to match. I became used to black dye on towels and basin and to the sight of Jill dashing down to the calf-shed, dark hair flowing, to compare with the bull-calf for blackness.

There was Drews, eating his cornflakes dry like a horse, whose blue eyes unaccountably vanished when he laughed and who, very much liked, came back to us for several summers; and another Richard who remains to me a second son although married now and living in Jamaica – to me all members of my family, and a part of the days of this farm.

# CHAPTER FOUR

BECAUSE there were no badger-cubs, my watches in the Valley that summer lacked much of the light entertainment that seems inseparable from watching young animals, whatever the species.

A vixen with a solitary cub beguiled some of my evenings. She had her earth in a secondary hole of the several that lead into the main badger sett, across the stream and exactly opposite from where I have made ledges for feet and sitting. (Vixens frequently share a large sett with badgers: in my experience they are not welcome, but are tolerated as long as they do not make themselves a nuisance.) At first this vixen would emerge well before the badgers, her one woolly cub close behind her, and she would sit for a while on the old badger-ramp that was her doorstep, the lonely cub bouncing around her. Over their heads a great beech-tree spread its low branches, and all around was the woodlands' own fence-to-fence carpet of warm russet beech-leaves.

Pardos was my most frequent companion of those summer watches: after he had taken to lying in wait for me at the Valley gate I gave up trying to elude him. He would sit with me up on the ledges watching with large round eyes the private affairs of the birds and deer, the badgers and the foxes. Generally he remained a fascinated observer, gazing, when the vixen had slipped away, at the solitary cub playing by itself for a little in a sober, solemn manner before going back into the earth; or at the badgers looking from their various entrances to test the scents and the sounds of the woodlands before emerging. But once a splendid cock pheasant stepped through the trees, all colours and swishing tail, and began slithering down the badgers' ramp to the stream below us.

Pardos goggled in his familiar wonderstruck manner, but when the pheasant flipped across the stream and began coming up our side it was too much. My Gingerbread Boy stared disbelievingly and then took off in a dashing charge – tilting his windmill as increasingly he seemed liable.

Uttering a loud horrified squawk the pheasant rushed into the ferns and undergrowth with Pardos crashing after him. There seemed little I could do except hope that nobody killed anybody. The squawking and crashing receded down the Valley and stopped. For five minutes even the birds were shocked to silence, and in the Valley there was only the sound of the stream. Then, sheepishly and slinkily, Pardos emerged from the fountains of male-fern, his ears swivelling as they did when he was embarrassed, and he came and sat again beside me. No violence seemed to have been done to him, and I trust none to the cock pheasant: Pardos and I by unspoken agreement did not refer to the matter again.

There was another time when the big boar badger looked out suddenly and early, making Pardos jump, so that he actually growled at him. To my astonishment the boar immediately retired and remained below for a full fifteen minutes. Pardos, who for some days had been lovingly teased as 'the cat who chased the roe deer and cock pheasant', now became 'the cat who growled at the boar badger'. Such a cissy, soppy cat he generally seemed, it was a contradiction of appearances seldom believed by those who didn't know him well. Towards the fox-cub he showed no reaction beyond what seemed like vague wonderment, sitting beside me watching its solitary little leaps and pounces as it played its lonely games among the ferns and foxgloves.

I had much hoped to see fox and badger cubs playing together, as I have heard sometimes happens, but first there was the absence of badger-cubs and then the growing intolerance between the badgers and the vixen. She did not do much to help the situation, once coming down so close to the badgers' quarters that the boar shot out and drove her away with ferocious growls. The following evening she was there again staring down at the sett, but the boar stayed below. She then barked sharply three times, but still he would not rise and finally she went back to her cub.

'She'll throw a stone next!' said Bill when I told him.

The next evening the boar was out before she was half-way down the bank between her beech-tree earth and the sett. There was a short fierce fight, during which Pardos clearly didn't know which way to run so stayed in horror beside me. Quickly the vixen saw where the power was and broke away to streak off into the woods.

The next night neither she nor the cub was there at the beech-tree. The badgers were out early, gathering leaves and bracken for bedding and scratching contentedly on their fortress platform, alone in their territory as clearly they wished to be. Pardos of course was with me. No terrors seemed ever to deter him from coming; not even the sudden appearance of two large strange dogs above us, one drizzly evening soon after the fight, when their approach had been muffled by wet leaf-mould.

I intended to discover where the vixen had now taken her cub, thinking that most probably she had gone upstream to another then disused sett known to my family as the Outlier, but tragedy forestalled me.

It was the evening of the strange dogs. Neither seeing nor scenting Pardos and me they had loped on up the Valley, their muzzles to the ground. Some ten minutes later there was a sudden outbreak of excited yelping of the kind that usually means a prey is somewhere cornered. It was in the direction of the Outlier. I feared for the cub, but now the barking was silenced and the light had nearly gone; Pardos was with me and there was nothing I could do that evening.

In the morning I took the stream path and followed it up to the Outlier – which is beyond our boundary on National Trust land – in steady rain and wind. I was alone, no cats wished for such a drenching.

It was as I had feared – at the entrance to the Outlier I found the cub, mauled and dead, a bedraggled little heap of russet fur. Thinking of the probable sorrow of the vixen I took the cub away; but perhaps we can never know how an animal really feels, or if we help or hinder when in any way we interfere.

Sometimes I was the one who was interfered with, but fortunately always with the best intentions. Although the Valley itself was our property the woods above to the west were not. Now and again someone would walk along there when I was watching, and sometimes I would be perceived as I sat huddled in the dusk, alone among the ferns. Occasionally the stranger would worry about this phenomenon and after passing return to stare and speculate. Was I some poor creature in trouble or despair? A potential suicide, perhaps? Someone on the run? Ill, or lost? Ought one to go down and find out?

Once or twice someone did, climbing carefully in the dusk down the steep wooded Valley side to my sitting ledge.

'Are you all right?'

'Yes. Sh! I'm waiting to see badgers. I often do.'

'Oh . . . It's rather a solitary occupation.' Pause. Then, inevitably, 'Why do you do it?'

'I suppose because it interests me. Please, will you be very quiet as you go?'

I had a real shock one night, which I think my friend David Walker will forgive me for relating.

As usual I was alone, and had not even a cat with me. The watching had been good and now it was too dark to see anything more; it was before the days when I accustomed the badgers to torchlight. Picking up my rubber pad I began moving along to the steps I had made down the steep bank to the stream-path. Then I noticed against the sky, high to my left, a man's figure standing still and watching me. It was too dark to see more than the black outline but I knew that he was there. Before I had reached the first of the steps he had begun moving down to me. Terror fluttered and died. A kind of cold fatalism took its place. There was no sense in running. Far from any house no one would hear me shouting; all I should achieve would be panic in the badgers.

The man had reached my ledge now and was coming along it. I stood there hung with binoculars, hearing my heart slamming and waiting for the unimaginable – a blow on the head? A quick knife in the ribs? – thinking in a hypnotized way, 'Well, sooner or later it must come to us all . . . '

Silently the man reached me. He was a yard away from me when he paused and leaned forward to whisper, 'Do you recognize me?'

Crazily, and to avoid disturbing the badgers, I whispered back, 'No, not in this light.'

There was a further pause before he leaned again to hiss at me, 'Strawberries!'

Now really I had someone mad to contend with, my fear convinced me. This would be worse by far than simple thuggery. And then again I heard the soft whisper, 'Is Dorcas still there?'

Those who have read my badger book will remember who Dorcas

was – the sow badger whom I watched so often with her cubs and her mate at this place. Relief flooded over me. And now I understood about the strawberries, and where my stranger-in-the-night would have come from. Seeing perhaps my state he went on to enlighten me – still in the badger-considering whisper; 'I'm Pat Coles's brother-in-law – where you come for strawberries. I read your book. Is Dorcas—'

'Yes, yes!' I answered, so delighted to be alive and in no fearsome peril. 'But no cubs this year. And – do please use my ledges if you like. They're more comfortable than standing at the top!'

Since that night David has often done so; sometimes on his own or when I am there, and we compare notes, the badgers not hearing a whispered conversation across the song of the stream.

'A roe buck in the woods last night,' he would say; or, 'The badgers were digging at the south hole.' And I would tell him about the foxes.

Sometimes when I did not go to the Valley I might be watching one of the lesser setts around the farm. There are several of these, none permanently inhabited as the main sett is but most of them used from time to time for short periods. I liked to walk around these setts in daytime to look for signs of occupation; fresh digging, tracks in soft ground, grass-blades trodden flat or recently used dung-pits – badgers do not dung indiscriminately but use a range of holes made for the purpose some distance from the sett.

One of the best of these outlying setts is in the hedge between Barn field and Lower Six Acres, only a field's length from the house but out of view of it. I liked to watch there, with my back against an oak-tree, whenever the signs were propitious, but interference here was really rife. It was still well-meaning but it came from cows, and the good intentions of cows do not promote the watching of wild animals. Rather they immediately proclaim, as with trumpets, the human presence.

Given some slight encouragement cows are friendly animals. Ours had always had a great deal of encouragement and were very friendly indeed. Besides being sociable animals cows are curious. First they like to find out what you are doing, and then to share in it; and when there are forty or fifty of them this is quite an experience. If the herd were grazing in this field I would sneak along the hedge with my camera and sitting-pad, keeping my face averted from the

A strange wild cat

Hula would hunt in all weathers

Settled on the ramp to groom each other

cattle – one glance at a cow is interpreted as an immediate invitation – and settle beneath my oak-tree.

All might be well for a few minutes, the herd grazing away from me, and I would begin to entertain my usual false hope that they would disappear into the next field and I should get away with it. But the grass in this field was rated high in their estimation, and presently one would turn and they would all turn, like flighting starlings, working towards me. Inevitably one would then see me and come and then all would come. There would be much blowing and sighing in my ear and gusting down my neck as the herd made sure that they knew me; then, cosily very close, they would begin to settle around me, shoving each other about for the best places. With groans and lurchings the successful would lower themselves, first at the knees and then the hindquarters. A few moments would be passed making themselves really comfortable – a heave, a thump, a kick, a swirl of the tail – and then business would be resumed as usual in the chewing of the cud. This peaceful and rhythmical occupation can sound loud if it comes into your ears at close range in multiple cow-power. There would be more sighings, and also belchings of decibels enough to please the most critical Arabs, with rumbles from each cow's four stomachs. Almost certainly I would presently be licked, industriously and with a noise like a file on wood, all the way up the back of my duffle-coat.

On such nights my hopes of seeing badgers were virtually nil: I might just as well have stood up and waved my arms and shouted to the cows to leave me. I used to wonder exactly why the badgers would not emerge. They could not have heard or smelt me. Did the gathering of sociable cows indicate to them that there must be an unusual cause, e.g. a human being? I don't think that this is attributing to them more reasoning than they could have, since many wild animals will take cover at the alarm-note of a jay or blackbird. Although in no way afraid of the bird itself, the animal knows that the alarm-note signifies the presence of an intruder.

On the other hand, were the badgers afraid of the cows? This may sound improbable to those who do not know our cows. Ever since the arrival twenty-two years ago of our foundation cow, Coronet, who was a great dog-chaser, our cows have all followed her example. No dog has ever been safe from them. Would the herd chase the badgers? I cannot say, as I have never had the luck to see cows and badgers together; but once I saw the whole herd in thundering pursuit of a vixen who streaked to the cover of a hedge, where the cows slid to a halt blowing heavily into the leafage.

In any case, unless the cows early left me I should see no badgers, and would finally go home in the dusk renewing my resolution to borrow from Bill a length of electric fencing to fence myself in – or out – from their good intentions.

# CHAPTER FIVE

THE year moved on into high summer, and the haying was finished, yellow hawkbit starring the dry grazings. Trellis was a sturdy little heifer (she would always be small) wolfing her calf-nuts, and Sean came home from university to leave us again almost at once on an expedition to the Azores.

The pullets had come through the gawkish age and looked like neat little coloured pigeons, their sleek new feathers in gorgeous variety according to kind: the two Welsummers were gold and golden-brown, like Chinese pheasants, with finely spangled ruffs; the Cream Legbars now displayed their rosy breasts and dove-grey wings – it seemed too much that such beautiful birds should also provide one with spring-green eggs and I could hardly wait for this bonus. Of the two Black Minorcas one had undergone a change of heart or hormones or something, and was growing a fountain of a tail. He also began to show a proprietary interest in the harem, but especially in the rosy-breasted pair.

My hennery was growing too big for folding over the lawns and Bill helped me to transfer the outfit to the big run in the Orchard. The Black Minorca unisex seemed now to decide what he was going to be and became known to us as Cocky: I kept him for his shining black splendour and pride, and because I hadn't the heart to think of an alternative fate for him. He revealed at once ideas about roosting. Where the harem took meekly to roosting in the hen-house provided, he fancied the cherry-tree that overhung it, and since he also fancied the rosy-breasted pullets he nightly enticed them up into its branches. They made a charming sight up there in the summer evenings, peering down from a bower of cherry-leaves, but I was afraid to leave them to the hazards of foxes and summer weather. Nightly I would climb up and reach for them, plucking them from the branches as one might pluck bright tropical fruits

(Cocky was bright, too, with his scarlet comb and wattles and white cheeks and the shine on his feathers), and put them one by one into the hen-house.

A new bird took our fancy that autumn; a wild cock pheasant who learned the goodness of hen-corn. Although a bold bird with Cocky and the pullets, floating into their run and pecking their corn from under their astonished faces, he was less bold with the heifers in the Old Orchard. Our dog-chasing herd thought pheasants a splendid quarry too, and would sweep after him with their tails aloft at the very first sight.

The pheasant would have done much better if he had not advertised himself so clearly. His approach to the heifers' fence was dignified, with slow and stately steps; but under the fence he would pause, look right, look left and, perhaps through nervousness, announce himself loudly. Immediately there would be a rout. Like a toy on wheels he would scuttle fast across the Orchard with the heifers in pursuit. He could perfectly well fly but would not do so, keeping just ahead of the heifers until he reached the safety of the opposite fence, where he would immediately slow down and resume his stately stepping.

He was not the only bird to appreciate hen-corn as the winter approached. I used to encourage a favourite robin and several hedge sparrows with small scatterings on an old churn-top, but the house-sparrows watched for me and came in squadrons when I appeared with corn-jug and basket. They would settle in clouds in the orchard trees, like a heavy crop of small brown fruit, and wait for me to scatter the corn. The chickens really resented this and would angrily chase the sparrows away, pounding after them with beaks open and wings flapping.

Friendly greetings from the pullets took much the same form. Whenever we returned from the shortest journey, if the chickens were out they would come rushing down the drive to meet the car, their wings wide and necks outstretched. It could be quite difficult to get into the garage without slaughter unless someone was there to call the chickens, Piper-like, to safer regions.

A strange wild cat came into our territory that autumn: not, of course a true wild cat, but a domestic tom gone wild. He was black, lean, long-haired and shaggy with the huge mats that come in these coats if uncombed. Probably he had never had a proper home; born in a barn or woodland he may have lived wild from kittenhood, hunting and scavenging where he could. Before he moved into our land we heard tales of him terrorising and beating-up the peace-loving local cats. The injuries he inflicted were deep and savage. One tabby of my acquaintance was going on three legs for some weeks; a ginger had a shoulder wound that could be seen from a distance, raw and red. Then suddenly the enemy was in our own country.

Hula and Pardos generally relied for their safety on their swiftness and agility and knowledge of the farm geography; but Old Force was not a cat to run away. Not only would he square up to the intruder but his power and authority – he was after all King in his own country – always prevailed, although sometimes not until cruel blows had been received and given. But we were worried about Mr Forsyte. He was getting older, and apart from this he had seemed lately not so well, sitting about in uncharacteristic quietness. Always a lean cat but full of muscle, he seemed perhaps leaner.

We did our best to drive away the wild cat, as indeed did all our neighbours – every man's hand was against him; but he had little to lose and continued his border invasions.

Inevitably there came a day when, overpowered by the younger assailant, Old Force turned and made for home; but not before the enemy had dealt a parting wound. There was nothing to be seen when Force came in, except his wrath and mortification, but he turned several times and licked quickly at the root of his tail. Then we saw that the tail was lifeless, trailing like a rope on the floor. He resented our inspection, and we could find only a small red tooth-mark, but clearly it had struck at the main nerve of the tail.

We called in our vet and he confirmed this, but offered us the hope that the paralysed tail could recover, although this he said might take some weeks. It was equally likely that the paralysis would be permanent, in which case the only measure was to dock the tail to avoid further injury from dragging.

While the vet was with us I had him make a general examination of the great old warrior, but he could find nothing amiss except his age.

'He is only ten,' I said, but I was reminded of what really I knew, that some animals – and people – age earlier than others and little is known about this matter.

From that day Bill carried a gun against the wild cat. So did the student, Ian. I saw, but said nothing. The injured in the area were mounting and now we had the first in our own home. It might be Hula or Pardos next, and Force was now vulnerable. But the wild cat was very elusive. Several times he drew fire but never was hit. No one was able to get near him. Sometimes we would see the ripple of his black form, belly to the ground, streaking through the grass or bracken to vanish without sound.

I tried to find out where he had come from, but nobody knew; he had just appeared.

Mr Forsyte continued to drag his beautiful black tail, and the hair underneath it grew thin although no soreness appeared. Sometimes he would snap round at it as if perplexed and annoyed at its lack of response to his direction, or its awkwardness in getting in the way when he wished to settle down. It had always seemed so mobile, as if it had a life of its own, waving gently when he was standing surveying the garden or lifting its tip when he sat by the Aga thinking. It had a kink at the end, in true Siamese tradition, and seldom was it still unless he were in the profoundest slumber.

I thought wistfully of how he would look with this splendid feature docked; and then one day, after about four weeks, I saw the end of it lift up – very slightly, but it lifted, clear of the ground. From then on the cure was swift; a little more movement every day, a little more swing and a little higher lift, until in another month one could not have known that the tail had ever been stilled.

Our rejoicings were brief, because now we began to see that Mr Forsyte truly was not himself. Daily he seemed to fade a little under our eyes, sitting by himself in a dream of detachment and eating less with less gusto. Again we called in our vet, and this time he made a fuller examination and told us that Force had diabetes.

No one will want to read of our sadness, of the searching discussions on insulin and what right we had, in his older years, to subject him to daily injections, and our decision to let him pass from us.

He lies in the farm garden under the orange azaleas, which flame no brighter than his great spirit had done. Sean and I were both in tears as we laid him to his rest. Never, I think, could a cat have been more loved but yet respected. Few can have had a fuller life, of fields and barns and wild woods and a warm welcoming farmhouse kitchen. He had an elegant mate and fine children, one of whom I daily greet as I leave the farm to go down to the village shop. To our family, as well as to many of our friends, he will always be remembered as The Greatest.

For some years we had had a cat-flap in the back door. The cats had used it in a confident if sometimes unorthodox manner. Hula was a great listener at the cat-door. As winter approached she would crouch under it listening for sparrows, who came down for the crumbs from the tablecloth – no amount of urging from me would make Bill or Ian shake the cloth further out, when I was away at tea-time. Judging her time to the half-moment Hula would suddenly project herself with a bang like a gun through the cat-flap, and fairly often she caught a sparrow. I thought this blind-hunting remarkably clever and efficient, but Hula is a clever and efficient cat. If the catch chanced to be a robin or a tit, however, we would grieve for it, and then I would begin debating with myself as to whether a sparrow were really of lesser value than a tit or a wren or robin. Life can be difficult for a realist who yet loves plants and animals. It is O.K. to cut down docks but not to trample bluebells: but are beautiful children more worthy of care than plain ones? And if it is a question of rarity, what about our own numbers?

In any event, the coming of the wild cat struck caution into the heart even of Hula in the matter of the cat-door. No one could be certain that the black one was not out there, waiting to pounce. While Hula dithered, Pardos was fairly terrified and would wait for us to open the big door rather than take a blind jump through the little flap.

'A window in the flap would make such a difference,' I said to Bill.

He had always intended to make one, but there is little spare time on a farm. The wild cat situation he rightly saw as urgent, may he be for ever blessed, and straight away he made and fitted a perspex window. The Burmese were enchanted, and from the beginning would spend hours sitting together on the doormat considering the world outside; looking with whiskers jittering at the birds, assessing the weather and the temperature and peering sidelong down the path for the wild cat. The flap now became known to us as the cats' television.

'Watching the box again; must be something exciting on,' Ian would say.

‘A natural history programme, I expect,’ Bill would tell him. ‘Something about birds.’

The window was and is a very great success, and I hope that the makers will take note and fit windows in their doors. No cat likes to take a leap into the dark, and ours now used the flap with perfect confidence.

When Sean was home one week-end that winter Hula lost a mouse behind the Aga. Anyone could see that she had lost a mouse there from the way she and Pardos were sniffing and peering, so Sean and I got a torch and peered for ourselves. There indeed was the mouse, sitting up with its nose and whiskers fluttering most engagingly. We decided to carry out a rescue and put Pardos and Hula into the sitting-room while we organized operations. First we opened the boiler-room door which is near the Aga, and then the outside door from there to the winter evening. With a bamboo section of the chimney-brush and squinting between the wall and the Aga I gently chivvied the mouse out at the far side, where Sean took over and herded it round the inglenook corner and into the boiler-room.

The round-up went slightly out of control here, our mouse overshooting the open back door and hurrying towards the big boiler behind which it could have gone to ground for ever. Sean put on speed and with some clever outflanking headed the mouse back and out into the night. We stood there in the doorway and watched it in the torchbeam, bobbling away down the garden, keeping to the path all the way as if obeying a notice, until it had passed from our sight.

I was reminded of an earlier mouse of Hula’s which got through to the stairs and so to my room where it found some suitable hiding place. I did not know about this until, in the middle of the night, I was awakened by something large in the jumble of my short hair. I sat up, switching on the light and shaking my head; to my amazement I saw a mouse fly out and land upon the carpet; it was a field-mouse, very pretty and engaging.

When it had come to itself it trundled across the carpet to the now closed door and sat up in front of it as if asking to be let out. So hypnotized was I by now that I got up to open the door, but the mouse ran to earth behind the wardrobe.

The next night, the mouse being hungry, I caught it in a device worked out by Bill and me; namely a bucket with cheese inside and a wooden gangway to the rim, where a short piece of cardboard was placed to tip when the mouse ran on to it. In this way I was able to take and release it outside.

The evening after the Aga mouse we discovered Pardos once more crouching by the back of the Aga watching in nearly the same place. Sean said, 'Oh, not again!' Closer investigation showed that the angle of Pardos's gaze was different, towards another gap just beside the Aga, viz., below a wooden ingle-seat which housed beneath it a jungle of central heating controls and on the top of it a stack of casseroles. Pardos's manner was authentically that of an anxious cat watching a lively and rather dangerous small animal; his head poking backwards and forwards to the presumed advances and retreats of the animal, his whiskers thrusting further by independent control, his eyes huge and very black.

We took out the armchair which stood in that side of the inglenook. We unstacked the casseroles and lifted the wooden seat, watched by our dithering but fascinated cat, and aimed our torch into the vitals of Bill's central heating.

No wild or other life revealed itself, but Pardos himself gave us our clue. Re-applying his eye to the crack in the seat-front he began again the advance-retreat neck and whisker movement; and we noticed, swinging in the draught in time with him, a mouse-sized curtain of cobweb hanging from a pipe.

We left the cobweb to amuse him with thrills of faint danger, and for several evenings he was to be seen there crouched at the gap and gently rocking in a slightly inebriate way.

The Aga was a constant attraction to our cats in the winter. For years I had been conditioned to cooking with cats sitting all around the saucepans on the insulated Aga-top, and although I felt that this could hardly be good for the cats or the cook I had never been able to devise a way of keeping them off. Now we had a new Aga, and the problem became intensified. The space left behind the open simmering-plate lid and the ingle-wall was less than on the old Aga; a raised hob was there with just enough room for a smallish cat to sit if he didn't breathe too deeply. Pardos had always favoured this place, and now continued to squeeze there. I thought this was really all right, but I hadn't allowed for sneezing. Twice he did this – pepper, perhaps, wafting to his nostrils – and each time the heavy lid came down with a crash on a simmering casserole. After the second time I saw that something must be done – the polished underside of the Aga-lid carried two deep half-moon dents and the casseroles remained slightly lop-sided after the most careful hammering treatment.

Accordingly Bill made two long beech-wedges to fit behind the hotplates. Hula, who as we knew could do anything, settled herself on the gradient once or twice, just to prove that it could be done; but Pardos was completely defeated, to the joy of all the itinerant cooks in our kitchen.

Keeping cats off the front and sides of the Aga was more difficult. I had earlier tried a two-pound polished brass weight but Mr Forsyte, who never noticed discomfort, simply sat on it, and one day according to Sean he 'hatched' it, the weight crashing to the floor and taking chips out of two tiles. Our final victory came after we brought in a pair of fourteen-pound ring-weights. People occasionally look in wonder at our Aga, with its beech-wedges and its two iron weights, and we have sacrificed the culinary uses of the hob area, but the advantages are worth it and the cats' coats have improved noticeably.

There was one slight contretemps when Force, abandoning his efforts to settle among the weights and wedges, retreated with a sigh to the usually despised cat-basket, in the left-hand corner of the inglenook and below the television shelf. But Hula was on the top of the set at that time, watching ski-ing, viewing as she always does upside down by leaning over from the top. Just then she was raking with a paw to catch the ski-ers, and this caused her to overbalance and fall into the cat-basket on top of Mr Force. Not unnaturally he was shocked and outraged, especially as Hula typically at once blamed it all on him, so that he left the basket seldom to return to it and no doubt felt that all places were closed to him; but we made it up to him with a special foam cushion, red on one side and black on the other, in the chair the other side of the Aga.

# CHAPTER SIX

DURING most of that winter the war went on against the wild cat, but always he eluded the guns and other missiles. His victims in the area continued to increase, but Pardos and Hula remained unscathed; she probably because of her quickness but Pardos, I could only think, by the unfathomable hand of providence, until I realised that the wildling had established his base in a woodpile at the edge of Yew Tree field and fairly close to the farmhouse. Foxes seldom kill near their own earth, the country saying has it – whether this may be to keep a reserve ration at hand or in the interests of secrecy I have not heard – so probably Pardos now had some special diplomatic immunity.

The wild cat himself was looking, to my increasingly sympathetic eye, more lean and ragged than in the spring and summer. Great lumps stood out from his long coat; we could see them against the skyline as he streaked along the headland of his roof-high territory. Bill thought that they were abscesses, resulting from fights and hard living. Whatever they were I worried about him, and the more as winter settled down. No one could ever get near enough to him to see properly; even with field glasses his elusiveness made viewing difficult; he always saw one first.

Reports of dreadful damage to other local cats continued to come to our ears, but as far as our two were concerned hostilities were definitely suspended. I began to wonder, since the hunters had failed to rid the area of the menace, if friendly overtures might possibly succeed. To my surprise Bill agreed to this. 'Give it a trial,' he said, and left his gun at home.

Then began my long months of enticement of the wild cat, for several weeks totally spurned by him. His main lying-up place still seemed to be the Yew Tree field woodpile, and he became known to us as The Woodpile Cat. This was the first of many names, more than any other cat connected with us has ever acquired. I began by leaving food for him at the midway point to the woodpile, and by making friendly noises whenever I caught a glimpse of him. The food was invariably rejected. Milk, meat, fish, brown bread and butter – all were ignored as if they simply were not there: no one at that time saw him even look at or sniff them. My sweet nothings – mouse-squeaks, puss-puss, pretty boy and the like – were treated as the most ominous threats and fled from immediately in his well-known belly-to-ground streak, his ears flat and tail rippling; he looked like some short black snake slithering swiftly through the grass.

There came a day towards spring when I saw him pause and look back for a moment as I called him. He had now acquired his second name, the unlikely cat-name of Rover. Although I usually called him by it, this was only a surname. The first name to it was Land, and he came by both because one day someone said, 'He does remind me of a Land Rover – his headlights are so close together.' (They are not really as we later discovered; it is only that his owl-ruff makes them seem so, but the name has stuck.) So there I was, in the Orchard on the way to feed the hens, when I saw him rippling through the grass and called, softly and enticingly, 'Rover! Rover, boy!' And for the first time he stopped and looked back at me, but then in a flash he was gone again, as ever before.

It was the beginning; a small one, but the beginning. In a day or so the spurned food was tentatively and with deep suspicion tasted. In a very few days more it was being wolfed with a mighty hunger. He had I suppose seen me put it there; presumably when I called to him in the fields he recognized in me the food-bearer, for now he would pause longer and swivel both his ears, even perhaps lifting his black banner of a tail before compulsively fleeing from me. Now he began coming closer to the house. Sometimes we would see him watching it, the coming and going of cats and people who obviously belonged and were wanted, and I thought even at a distance that I detected a wistful look.

Hula and Pardos were disturbed and apprehensive about his closer orbit, and I too was anxious of the possible outcome of a confrontation, for Rover was a large and powerful cat, and his leanness was giving way to my feeding. But the diplomatic immunity was never violated. The outlaw would only stand and watch, his ears and tail slowly waving, whatever the Burmese provocation of growls and hissing.

There was a day when he crept so close that he stood behind the lily-tub opposite the back door; and he stayed there as very slowly I came out and approached him, stooping to his level and talking nonsense, but he was on the very edge of flight. Finally I extended a slow finger from my side of the tub; and – wonders – in a long suspicious stretch he extended his muzzle: but his ears were flat down to his head as if he had been born without any. So it was that we first made contact, the Woodpile Cat and I. He was gone, of course, in a flash of mistrust; but soon he was back again.

I began feeding him on the back terrace at the same time as the Burmese in the kitchen. Several times I was warned by friends and family, and often I was apprehensive, but I was pulled over by compassion for this outcast. On cold nights especially I felt pity for him, as once or twice I saw his face wistful outside the window in the cat-door, looking inside at the warm comfort of the lighted kitchen, the home cats curled against the Aga and people sitting at their books or writing around the big table. But whenever we went to open the door he would vanish at once into the rain and dark.

Once contact had been established, without wound on either side, progress was swifter than we had imagined possible. Rover now knew the meal-times and always reported for them, peering from behind the lily-tub. One by one the members of our household announced, 'I've touched him!' My own fraternization advanced through conversational channels to stroking and a rub behind the ears, until ultimately I told the impressed household, 'I've picked him up!'

He was so rigid in my hands that he felt like a wooden cat. He was not as heavy as we had thought, his ribs gaunt under the fingers, his seeming bulk due to the mass of his coat. I was glad to reassure myself that the lumps were indeed not abscesses but fur-mats, with which I could deal in the course of time, and then I put him down again on his own legs to calm his rising panic.

Natalka was staying with us that spring. Nicholas and Natalka are citizens of the world, especially the Mediterranean world where – both of them marine archaeologists – they spend their summers in search of sunken cities; but on visits to us Natalka has always been just a member of our farm family, involved in any activities that may be going on. Never really a cat-person – the first time I visited her she fascinated me by rising from dinner to catapult with a spoon from the table a tom cat that had ventured into her garden – she became involved with Rover.

Natalka was brought up with horses and dogs in Poland. She has what is known as a 'way' with them, indeed probably with all animals; certainly with our cats and cattle to a degree which I cannot equal. I early discovered this when, losing the struggle to get a big tape-worm tablet down Hula – a chain rabbit catcher – Natalka took this fierce little fighter and popped the tablet down like a coin into a slot machine. No force, no violence, no struggling, just the enviable 'way' which, like artistic talent, presumably one is born with.

Whenever Natalka was here, and there were awkward animals to dose or attend to, we called her in as a kind of resident vet and watched her do easily what usually was a tricky thing for two of us. She was naturally the one to deal with Rover's coat. Every morning, his garden breakfast finished and he sitting now in front of the lily-tub – a great step forward as he was there in full view of the kitchen – she and I would sit on the terrace beside him, and I would tickle him behind the ears while she – apparently nonchalantly – took comb and scissors to the appalling tangles in his coat.

Our family has never cared for long-haired cats. Like odd-shaped dogs they seem too far removed from the basic shape to be either pleasing or practical; but from the beginning of our real acquaintance Rover was so disarming that all of us fell for him. We endlessly and frivolously argued among ourselves that really he wasn't a cat at all, and speculated as to what animal he might be.

'A musk-ox; no other animal has a coat like that, fairly sweeping the ground and that colour – unless it's an ant-bear?'

'What about an Oliphaunt?' said someone who was reading *The Lord of The Rings;* 'only the trunk is at the other end. Or do you think really he's a Balrog? Or the Dark Lord himself?'

Sean held that we would never really know what animal he was until we could see 'what was inside all that fur', but the chances were, he said, that he was a dog, since all Rovers were dogs, unless they were cars or footballers which clearly he was not.

He began now to come to our call, which was usually, 'Hey! Rover!' And so he acquired a hyphen and the nickname of Hey-

Rover; his proper first name, Land, seemed never to catch on. He kept always a dignified distance from the two Burmese, averting from their agitated neck-cranings his strange pale-gold eyes that were the shape of D-rings fallen forwards. His coat now looked very peculiar; of flowing length it quickly took on a high shine where it existed, but here and there – where the tangles had been – there was a kind of clearing in the lushness, as if a mad scytheman had got loose in a field shut up for hay. He had – and of course still has – down the middle of his back a parting extending along the length of his tail, another feature in common with the little musk-ox; and so luxuriant was his underneath fur that his perfectly normal legs hidden inside it reminded me of castors underneath a sofa.

Now he would announce himself from a distance, mewing plaintively as he approached the house, while our two watched through the cat-window as though he had been a wolf seeking whom he might devour; until before their thunderstruck faces he would roll over kittenishly, his huge paws grasping the air.

Since Rover was now ranging and hunting in the farm buildings which had always been Hula's ratting territory, rather than risk a confrontation she opted right out and switched her line to rabbits. True to her character of doing anything better than anyone else she showed a finesse in this line which far excelled her skill with rats. I have recorded for her first month, April, 15 rabbits, this figure reaching 41 by June 10 and soaring to the improbable total of 74 before the end of August; and this in post-myxomatosis times. One has to remember that she is a tiny cat, no bigger than a medium-sized rabbit herself. She would hunt in all weathers, sometimes ranging the fields when it was too wet for most rabbits to be out and returning soaked trace-high, not always empty-handed.

On those spring evenings it was still cool enough for us to be glad to light the log fire in the sitting-room and play music on tape or record, while others perhaps who preferred it stayed box-watching in the big kitchen. Sometimes when Natalka could be lured into her magical tale-telling we would turn the lights and music softer to listen. Never have I known anyone who could hold so enchanted the listeners to tales of funny and splendid and desperate and heroic events as Natalka can. Nor have I ever known anyone who in less than half a lifetime has packed such drama.

'Have I told you about the night I spent sleeping on the dead engine-driver?' she might begin, and away we are launched on some terrifying saga of war-time Poland – the split household, the burnt house, the lost horses and acres. 'I was brought up to violence,' she will say in her gentle voice when our eyes express our horror. 'Some things I couldn't tell even to you.'

Out of the ruin and loss and torment Natalka made her way to England, and there through many vicissitudes and in a second language and with only a governess education behind her, to university, and now is an M.A. of Cambridge. She reminds me very much of Hula – small, feminine, efficient and quite indomitable.

Once I said to her, ashamed of writing so much about our humdrum Edwards lives; 'It is you who should be writing autobiography.'

'It would hurt too many people,' she said, and taking his brush and comb went to look for Hey-Rover.

The cowshed swallows raised their broods

Natalka on Copper

The sow and her cubs came out

The fox-cub alone in the Valley

# CHAPTER SEVEN

THAT spring, after two blank years, three cubs were born to the badgers in the Valley. There were too more singing birds, the dawn chorus beginning to reflect a little of its splendour in the earlier years, before the woods fell so silent that a friend returning after a long absence asked, 'What has happened to all the birds?'

Our small experience of the Silent Spring was more than I cared for. It was wonderful to see the birds and young animals returning, although still there were no nightingales or nightjars, birds which had once beguiled my evenings. I had watched for many milder nights of winter and spring before I knew for certain about the cubs. There had been much digging out of the ancestral breeding sett – but so there had in the cubless years – and much bed-gathering – but so there had in every year and season.

On one of these nights, March 21, there was the unusual combination of moonlight and warm weather. Sitting in comfort on the made-to-measure ledges opposite the main sett, and protected by three layers of warm socks and jerseys and a duffle-coat over, I gave myself to the pleasure of the peaceful Valley woods under the half-moon.

The badger pair, of whom Dorcas was one, came up at 8.40 G.M.T. When they had reassured themselves, as they always must, that the woods at least to windward were free of enemies, they relaxed and settled on their rampart to groom each other's coats. This was done with mutual appreciation and I am sure affection, the neck stretched up and the occasional rubbing muzzle, before they began to play together like cubs; and then still together they went away into the woods.

Soon they were back, and for the first time I noticed something quite contrary to what is accepted as normal badger behaviour. As they returned through the moonlit trees I saw clearly that the boar was carrying something in his mouth. The details were obscure but the size and shape and limpness were those of a dead rabbit. According to the experts badgers, unlike foxes, do not take food of any kind home, and never down into the sett. Dorcas's mate took his burden underground, she following, and there they stayed.

This seemingly unimportant incident of badger life interested me extremely – even I suppose thrilled me, as small exceptional incidents will always thrill watchers of wild animal behaviour. As it happened it was to come more sharply into focus as events of subsequent springs threw light on it. At that time I was not absolutely certain that the burden was a rabbit, and my reading led me to suppose that it could not be so.

I sneaked away silently while the pair were underground.

On April 23 I saw the first cub – just the small striped head close by the sow in the north entrance – and then it was gone again. Dorcas sat down and began grooming herself, and gradually all three cubs emerged. She spent a long time cleaning them all close by the entrance while I watched enchanted, and wished that I were near enough for a photograph; but I seldom moved in close with the camera now because of the disruption that it always caused in the badgers' peaceful life.

The cubs were playful, squeaking and yikkering as they rolled and bounced together. One lost its balance on the rampart edge and fell, rolling over and over right down the steep bank to the stream. The sow went anxiously after it and nosed it back up to the sett again. I watched until it was too dark to see, and then crept away while I could still do so without using a torch. Wood anemones and delicate oxalis were everywhere shining dimly in the dusk, and I knew that violets now invisible were with them. Roe deer were running in the woods around me and I could hear fox-cubs; a cuckoo and a tawny owl called somewhere in the very young leaves, but I missed the nightingales. When we first came here five pairs were nesting on our farm.

There were again fox-cubs in the beech-tree hole above the main sett, where the solitary cub had been the spring before; but this time there were five. I was concerned about them after last year's fight and its disastrous consequences. As the evenings passed I grew more anxious because the boar badger was clearly intolerant of their junketings, and five fox-cubs make a great deal more noise than one.

Inevitably, it seemed, there came the evening of the big fight, and perhaps inevitably too the defeat of the vixen who left with her five cubs and a bleeding ear. For another spring I was not to see this marvel of the two kinds of cubs playing together; and not I think because of any antipathy on the cubs' part but perhaps more a kind of universal insularity of parents who will not let their children play with others not approved.

The vixen went this time to a true fox-earth in Inner Wood, and there recovered from her torn ear and reared four of her cubs without disaster.

Rover's trust and friendliness seemed to expand with the leaves and flowers of that spring. He understood now that he was of the clan, if yet a fringe member. The day I really knew this was when, early in the spring, I went walking through the fields as usual to the Valley with Pardos and Hula, and half-way I turned to look at my two following cats and found that I had three, for several paces behind the Burmese was Rover. This was the first time in his life, I should imagine, that he had followed rather than run from a human being.

As the back door began more to be left open, the more he ventured inside it; a cautious step at first, and then another, until in a few days he was sitting on the doormat. Here he would trill sweetly across the kitchen to Hula, who much enjoyed it, but to the fury of Pardos – 'chatting up my woman' – who yet knew his limitations and made no move save glowering.

Rover would not come in through the cat-flap, but in the early mornings when the door was opened he would come walking across the lawn, his huge paws – dew-wipers, Bill called them – sweeping a swath in the wetness. Of a hairiness I have never seen equalled his paws sprout fur between and even under the toes: he would now pause uncertainly and pound the stone path with them as morning greetings were exchanged; then, reassured, he would advance again with rising hope and confidence, walking in his own individual way with both legs on the same side together, in the manner of an American pacing-horse.

He would now sit on people's knees, but very anxiously and ready to leap away the moment our hold on him was slackened. We had always to take great care because if he were suddenly excited or frightened his wildness would break out and he would slash with the scimitars he kept sheathed in all that hairiness. All of us, even Natalka, carried a few scars. We had to be especially careful when he was rolling kittenishly with his feet in the air; the temptation to tickle that furry tummy was considerable but we soon learned to resist it. Our flippant theory was that when he was turned topsy-turvy his feelings were, too; all his old suppressed violence coming up to the top again.

One great thing happened because of Rover that spring; I am almost certain that just by his presence the cowshed swallows raised and launched their three broods without disaster for the first time since Hula had come to the farm. Always she had watched and waited until the young swallows were fledged, and then she had climbed the concrete wall and into the rafters as only she could do and taken all. Spring after spring it had happened, do what we could to protect them; until this spring when Rover was hunting in the cowsheds and she had abdicated to the fields and woods. Rats not swallows were his quarry; he could never have reached the nests with his bulk and clumsiness, even had he wanted to do so.

As often in dry springs we had made mud-puddles for the swallows to use for nest-building, and Bill had made a supporting ledge for a nest that showed signs of crumbling. Now, when he was milking, the swallow family would roost on the overhead pipeline, leaning down to peer with interest – now with this eye, now with that – at his passage among the cows and their coming and going. The joy and feeling of achievement (although the achievement was not ours) in seeing the young birds safely in the air was such that we broached a bottle of year-old mulberry wine and drank the health of all concerned.

Wine-making breaks out as a recurrent crisis in this house. Now suddenly the dandelions were blazing and Natalka and I were out in the sunshiny fields picking the little golden suns around our ankles. While we were in the middle of this came the day of the swarm.

For years Bill has had a row of white hives in the Orchard. No one seemed ever quite sure how many there were, and I think Bill himself was a little vague about it. As the herd and the acres had grown he had found less time for the bees, and no one else showed any enthusiasm. Sometimes we had honey in the autumn and sometimes we did not; this depended on many things, such as the weather, the pressure of farm work, offers of help and the kind of summer it had been.

On this blazing afternoon in late May I went up to wash dandelion stains off my hands and found my room full of bees. From a fairly safe place behind the door I ascertained, (a) that they were swarming in my chimney and, (b) that such hundreds as fell into the room could not get out via the open windows because ye olde windowes in this ancient house do not open at the top, and bees always fly to the highest light place. (It must not be thought that I am exaggerating in saying hundreds: 15,000 bees, says Bill, constitute a smallish swarm.)

I left the scene quickly and hurried to report my predicament to Bill; but Bill, I found, was extremely busy thinking about starting to cut for silage. I took my problem to Natalka, who after all had taken her degree in zoology, although not, she clearly told me, as much in relation to bees as to sticklebacks and lemmings.

I know now, but did not then, that it is the easiest thing in the world to interest Natalka in anything. Her mind avidly seeks more things for study and experiment. Anything one might be doing – chutney-making, gardening, woodwork, wine-making – she is likely to take up and master, all much more scientifically than I with graphs and charts and check-tests. My bee crisis triggered her off at once, as I had hoped it would. In minutes we were braving the doom-cloud in my room and attempting to block the light from the top windows. We failed in this for reasons of medieval house construction, and Natalka called for a ladder, meanwhile lighting little smudge-fires in old tins salvaged from the dustbin and setting them in my fireplace.

In the end I had to apply to our lifelong friends the Loarridges at Cosford Mill for a ladder both long enough and safe enough. Himself a bee-keeper John Loarridge came with the ladder and various other useful equipment, including a bee-smoker and a straw skep, and gave his evening to my rescue. I admit that I hovered uselessly and Bill industriously milked while John puffed his smoker in my fireplace and Natalka made an assault up the outside chimney via the ladder to plant the bee-skep (her flag of conquest) on the summit.

By nightfall there still seemed to be an odd thousand or so bees in my bedroom but John and Natalka were fairly well pleased, as generals who at least have held off a serious attack. I was reassured that bees would not savage me in the night and that they would all be in the skep by early morning and ready for taking.

By this time Natalka had decided that bee-keeping would be interesting and therefore she would do the taking. This roused a small jealous response from Bill, just in from milking, and he explained to her how hazardous – even foolish – it is for someone with no experience at all to start up in keeping bees. This of course fired Natalka's enthusiasm, and both of them went up the chimney. Shortly they shot down again throwing off clothes in the kitchen, and Sean and I were urgently required to extract embedded stings with razor-blades. Natalka had fifteen and Bill more than fifty.

There was much dabbing of this and that special remedy and – very late – everyone finally went to bed; I in much doubt and fear and determined to be up before my bedfellows were aroused by daylight.

A wind blew up in the night. Around dawn as I was weighing in my mind the discomforts of early-rising against the agonies of multiple stinging I heard a dull crash in the south garden. The skep, I thought, and inspection proved that it was so. Distracted bees in their thousands crawled over, in and around it as it lay like an abandoned basket on the lawn.

Bill rushed past it to the early milking.

'Well, I think I leave it to you,' I said cravenly to Natalka, stifling my frightened yawns. 'I'll make some coffee.'

All Natalka's life has been a drama. Crises are her breath and the essence of her normality. I think in states of peace and order she is not fully alive. There was a quick conference in the cowshed – the generals discussing action. From my window I could see Natalka checking churn contents and Bill washing udders. Farms are like theatre; the show must go on – milk-flow and the milk-lorry wait for no man.

I suppose I was useful in getting the breakfast but I felt a little mean as Natalka, alone against a swarm of angry bees, rigged up a hive on the lawn, calling for a sheet and some honey. She was now wearing Bill's old bee-veil and his long white gloves, but the veil, I knew, was darned and unbeeworthy. She was searching through the enemy ranks when I brought the equipment.

'Do you know what the queen looks like?'

'Bigger and sharper,' I told her.

Natalka spread the white sheet for the bees to walk up from the skep to the hive (this is the proper procedure) and laid a honey-trail to encourage them. Breakfast was accompanied by bee-books and bee-talk, and the occasional glazed expression that comes to one who has suddenly felt a bee against the skin somewhere and is about to leap up and start banging at or throwing off a garment.

Natalka hived her bees and took them home in the back of her van, as we knew that she would do.

A new small swarm settled in my chimney that afternoon, but I lit my smudge-fires in their dustbin tins at once and they dispersed without trouble.

# CHAPTER EIGHT

HIS interest revived by these events Bill went up to the top of the Orchard and looked at his bee-hives – neglected, overgrown by bracken and tilted by pushing heifers. They were too far away, he told us, for a busy farmer to look after them. If I hadn't objected to having them near the garden they would have been at hand and properly managed and there would have been much honey stored in the attic. Now he proposed to bring them nearer, and if I found them a nuisance I needn't write in the garden: there were other places for me but not for the bees if he was going to look after them.

When Natalka returned that evening she had made a bee-veil for herself, and very fetching she looked in it; like an Edwardian motoring lady, full of mystery and half-hidden charm, with a certain forbidding formality.

Sean and I were very careful to keep ourselves occupied with our film developing and typing and so forth while the generals once again conferred and went into action. There were, it transpired, to be night manoeuvres, as the enemy was notoriously torpid in the dark hours. The plan was to capture their hives one by one and carry them bodily with their sleepy squadrons to new territory in Yew Tree field just above the house.

As soon as darkness settled the operations began. Too fascinated to ignore them completely, Sean and I went out from time to time to look on the strange night processions down the Orchard: Natalka and Bill both mysteriously clothed and veiled in what might be taken for priestly garments, appearing at measured intervals in the half-moonlight and bearing between them on clothes props a hive shrouded in white sheeting. It was like some sinister midnight burial, of the Ku Klux Klan perhaps. As the cortège passed through the garden we could hear from deep within the shrouds a dynamo hum.

From time to time there were urgent shouts for assistance, as a hive slipped on its stretcher and threatened to crash, or old sections began to disintegrate; and soon there was the familiar spectacle of Bill and Natalka dashing into the kitchen with haloes of angry bees and flicking out stings with razor-blades. Although admiring of so much courage – and even we said to each other foolhardiness – Sean and I kept to our peaceful pursuits and helped only when life would seem to have depended on it.

The eleven hives were all finally transported to the Yew Tree site, and the bee period settled into a fairly peaceful era with Bill and Natalka restoring and painting old hives and reading to each other and us all from bee-books.

We had staying with us that summer Jill and Riki. Jill was here to take over the milking for a few weeks and Riki, visiting from Hamburg, just for fun and anything else that happened. Our interest sometimes flagged in the bee revival and the readings from the great authorities, and when this happened Natalka would infuse fresh zest into our meal-times with breathless chew-stopping tales of death and disaster.

Around this time Riki broke out in chicken-pox. The rest of us reckoned ourselves immune, except Bill who said he didn't remember ever having it, so he took himself into solitary confinement in the caravan. There was no umbrage involved; on the contrary I think that he enjoyed it. He would come down at meal-times and sit with Rover beside the lily-tub, looking in through the open door and asking plaintively if we had anything for the man in the caravan. Naturally he always got the best the kitchen could offer and, as Amanda was with us again, often a choice of attractive females to bring it out for him, as well as to paint and repair the caravan. There was even talk of making him some curtains, but I am afraid this good intention failed to mature and he was obliged to tack up fertilizer bags.

With Jill in the house the familiar neats-foot oil stains began to reappear on the kitchen table as she set about her old spare-time task of mending and restoring our collection of old harness and tack. She was delighted that we still had, hanging in the kitchen, the little bridle which, when a student here, she had made from plaited binder-twine for her Angus bullock, and this too had to be washed and polished. Horse-talk began to rise through the bee-talk and in this field Natalka could hold us more enthralled even than by war and disaster. 'Did I tell you about when I found my black stallion, Steppe, kneeling on the stable-lad and tearing off his clothes? You had to know that horse: he used to dance on one leg screaming and waving the other three in the air; but he was a good horse.'

Suddenly we were all taken by an old longing. It was unthinkable that there was no horse at Punch Bowl Farm, where horses had been the children's school transport, our first farm power and my means of village shopping and ranging over all our wild countryside. I came to hear of Copper, a pony with problems which I understood because I shared them: he both hated and feared heavy traffic. Few people have riding country to suit such an animal. His honest owner, Naomi, when she wanted to part with him for an easier pony, would not conceal his character from inquirers. In this way he came to us on long loan. He was a handsome chestnut with a strange blaze that broke above the muzzle, so that he looked as if he were wearing a head-collar. He was so fat through lack of exercise that his girths would not meet, and riding him bareback was like sitting on a beach-ball in a choppy sea.

I did not have much chance to exploit this sensation because, although Natalka and Nicholas were now away again – in Greece if I remember – Riki and Jill and Amanda and even Sean so continually rode and schooled him that he melted and sobered visibly. Amanda and Jill liked best to set out on long rides through the woods around the Bowl, sometimes arriving in Hindhead and visiting shops, where once Copper raided an outside fruit-stall and only his escorts' charm and beauty put things right. Riki was not used to bare-back riding, although very able in the saddle, and would experiment in this around the farmlands. I think Copper appreciated his leisurely strolls with her in contrast to his adventures with Jill and Amanda, or perhaps Riki's gentleness influenced him; he was sweeter with her than with anyone.

'He is so kind,' she once told me in her German-English; 'when I get off for a gate, and cannot jump on the first or second time because of his fatness, he waits and waits.'

She discovered in him a fastidiousness, too, that none of the rest of us had given him time to show. 'He is so delicate, he does not like treading in the patches that the cows make; he peers down at them with his ears, and walks round.'

Jill used him as a cow-pony, collecting the cattle for milking or herding them down to the Punch Bowl fields which are far from the farm. One would see the familiar bikini and gumboots on the round spread of Copper's barrel, and the black hair and chestnut mane blowing as drumming hoofs drew one to the window.

After Jill had left to take up a horsy job in Ireland we found ourselves compelled to think up another way of getting the herd to and from the Punch Bowl. I was too busy to offer my regular services as cowgirl, and Riki and Amanda soon were gone away.

The long Wagon Track that Bill had made down to the Bowl was already fenced and gated. To me it is the most beautiful road that I have seen in all my life. Its surface is of the natural peat-soil of the woods through which it winds, silent and kind to human or equine foot. It carries no sight or sound of traffic, except the very occasional tractor or Land Rover, and it is lapped on the one side by heather and bracken hills where deer may spring out, and on the other by ancient oak woods that overhang and shade it as they fall to the jingling stream, Smallbrook.

Bill made this track where a very old way used to be, in the distant days when the Broomsquires (from broom-squarers: they were makers of birch-brooms) lived in the now-ruined Punch Bowl cottages: it was the school-path for their children, winding some two or three miles to the village but long ago engulfed by the woods and bracken.

In the early mornings and late evenings I would often take Copper and ride down the track to talk to Mr Watkins, the retired National Trust ranger, who lives in a perfect ancient cottage just where the track turns into the Punch Bowl fields. He it was who solved our cow-escorting problem, and his system worked perfectly. All that it involved was our turning the herd into the Wagon Track after the early milking and his closing the gate behind them as they filed into the fields at the entrance beside his cottage. At four o'clock he would open the gate again and see them off back up the track, where the thought of dairy-nuts and the easing of full udders would bring them home without need of an escort.

Mr Watkins enjoyed this self-imposed task. He had taken an interest in the herd from the time they first began going to the Bowl fields; he had his favourites and we often talked about them as I sat on Copper's broad back at his gate, but he liked to keep a watchful eye on the whole herd, telling us if one looked as if she might be near calving, or another walked a little lame, or was not 'quite right' in any way.

'Now, Quince there, she's my favourite,' he would say, picking her out in the far field with his blue seaman's eyes (he had seen war service in the Royal Navy). 'She'll always try anything on; adventurous and inquisitive, that's what she is. If there's a gate unlatched, or a weak place in the hedge, she's through it.'

'I think Ginkgo has the edge on her for character,' I would argue; 'the way she dances round the tractor until she turns the front wheels – and that really does make her dance! And the luscious noises she makes when she's waiting for her nuts.'

Mr Watkins would ignore my faulty partisanship. 'There's Traveller; now she's a great talker – talks to you all the time. She can open the gate, too, if I'm not there in time. The others just wait for her to do it. Dewdrop, she's another one I like. She follows you about, she's a sociable cow.'

There was one cow in his life whom Mr Watkins hated. A Jersey but not one of ours she was called Hide-and-Seek, and once she hooked him with her horn as he was walking home through her field with his bread in a rabbit-net over his shoulder. He always knew her among the others, he told me, and if she challenged he would 'bring her down' by a grip and twist above the hock, 'as wolves do'. He always had interesting tales to tell, as we paused at his gate, and I would check the dancing pony who fretted to be off, and Mr Watkins would give him the peardrop he always looked for and expected.

'Found an adder over there by the stream,' he said once. 'I lifted it up by the tail and, do you know, it coughed out a toad! That toad's luck was in – just in time – it hopped away back to the stream.'

Another day it might be deer.

'There's a fallow doe with a fawn in the new plantation. There is most years. I used to wonder how the fawn got in, because she takes it there after it's born. Then I saw. She nosed it up over the wire-netting and then jumped in after.'

Mr Watkins lives alone, now that his daughters are grown up and away from home (he brought them up himself, after his wife was killed in an air raid on Portsmouth). He has kept many animals at his cottage by the stream – dogs, foxes, ferrets, hens, a mynah bird – and we like to talk about them. His two dogs Punch and Trigger had a running feud with the mynah.

'Do you remember how the mynah used to call the dogs in?' I would ask him.

'My lord, yes! They never learned. Always rushed in. "Punch! Trigger! Where have you been?" That bird said it as clear as I do. Punch, he would pull every feather out of him if he could get hold of him.'

I used to appreciate the expressive wolf-whistle from the mynah when I appeared suddenly at the door.

'Now Punch, he was a good one for catching and shaking adders. Shook one once that whirled off and wrapped round Trigger's neck! I tell you. Poor Trigger rushed away, chased by Punch and scared of the adder; but it just fell off. He was a funny dog, Punch,' Mr Watkins would add reflectively. 'He would tolerate all liberties in the house and garden. I had a squirrel once that scolded and stamped on him! And he'd lick little rabbits; but the moment they stepped out of the garden they were legal prey.'

I told him about the large fox-cub I had seen, playing alone in the Valley, up and down the badger paths and sniffing at the setts; how it had gone down into the main sett, to my apprehension, and stayed there a full minute before running out with the old boar close behind it. 'He was on the cub's trail with his nose to the ground, although he was only a few yards behind. The cub slipped into the stump hole and the boar followed. Then both shot out of the lower hole – 50 yards away – and into the woods. The old man was back about half an hour later – I hope the cub was all right – and the sow and her cubs came out, and they all played together until I went home. It was very cold and starry.'

'Ah, yes,' said Mr Watkins. 'It beats the box, doesn't it?'

# CHAPTER NINE

As the summer went on, Rover the Woodpile Cat grew bigger and heavier and more trusting. He seemed to have an infinite capacity for eating, now that he had come to accept our offerings, and we had to be careful that he did not get too much. He had strange preferences, relishing things like cabbage and runner beans – he is the only cat I have ever heard of to make himself sick from a surfeit of boiled cabbage, but that was before we realised how carefully he had to be rationed.

Once or twice I found him sitting with Hula in Yew Tree field above the farmhouse and hoped Pardos would not notice. He came confidently into the kitchen now and was pleased to sit on knees, though in a cautious and watchful way; otherwise he always chose a hard chair – as if better for emergency take-off – in contrast to the cushion-opulence preferred by the Burmese; or he would settle on the tiled kitchen floor, usually close to a chair or table-leg as if tied to it by an invisible tether. His long coat, daily brushed and combed now, grew fine and glossy; it was not fluffy, as it had seemed when choked with matted underhair, but with a texture like raw silk, and having a faint crinkliness that showed clearly in photographs.

During the late summer Rover learned to play. He had clearly never discovered this activity before; it was as one might say a completely new field of study – as of course was the whole subject of friendly human relations in his world of hard knocks and hostility. A ping-pong ball tossed for him by Sean was plainly a missile and Rover went straight through the cat-door – an accomplishment he had been careful to master at an early stage. We saw that all playful overtures had to be very slow and gentle until confidence was firmly established. It was a delight to teach him these arts, and he became a fascinated and facile pupil, goggling with wide black eyes at the feather wiggling on a string or the ball of paper crumpled for his pleasure.

He took a fancy to newspaper and would lie on it if anywhere accessible. He loved to tear it up, rending it savagely with teeth and claws as if working out some buried psychosis. Until we came to terms with this temptation we were obliged at times to read the news like a jig-saw puzzle, swapping vital pieces round the table.

For a time Rover had to submit to fairly frequent flea-powdering, this partly because we only attempted small areas at a time of his abundant coat. Buying fresh supplies of dusting powder we discovered that this is now scented in a very sophisticated way. 'Why does your wild cat smell of talcum?' I was asked by a friend shortly after a session.

Rover would now follow me anywhere and if I went out of the room he would call to me plaintively until he established where I was. If I were going to the chickens, to the garden or the Valley, he would be padding at my heels. Sometimes on a known path he would trot ahead, his silky coat fairly flowing in the breeze, the long parting revealing itself from his shoulders to the end of his feather-boa tail. We used to say to each other, 'Isn't it a shame that we've never liked long-haired cats? But Rover is different, of course. Good dog, Rover!'

Hula had no prejudices about long-haired cats, whether they were really dogs or not. Taking advantage of his interest in her she would show off quite outrageously, playing with sunbeams or wisps of hay in front of him or rushing up the kitchen window in her well-known way to disappear into the roof or Sean's bedroom, leaving Rover gazing upwards, completely mystified.

Pardos took a disapproving view of Rover's fascination with his mate, and would sometimes make a very frank statement on the matter. He was too much aware of the wild cat's physical superiority to provoke a real show-down, but at a safe distance he would square up, asserting his rights, and having said his piece let the matter drop.

I saw, however, that something must be done fairly soon about what was known as the Indoctrination of Rover, or there might well one day be blood-letting over Hula. I rang our vet about it and arranged the date, with warnings as to what kind of patient Rover might be, supposing that we ever managed to get him to the surgery at all. The cat-basket, to say nothing of car, town and surgery, were outside all his experience. He might very well tear a basket completely to pieces, I thought, and then hold the driver at tooth-and-claw-point; we didn't know. I therefore borrowed from Mr Watkins a strong reinforced basket which he used for transporting ferrets, and beguiled Rover into it.

My fears were needless. Total silence prevailed in the basket on the twenty-minute drive. Rover had died of fright, I decided anxiously, but a peep through a ventilation hole was countered by his yellow D-shaped eye. He appeared to be pondering this further new experience and regarded me with a kind of trusting wonderment. I felt mean as I handed the basket to my vet.

When I went back later to collect him I asked how he had behaved, while noting with relief the absence of plasters on the veterinary fingers. 'Oh, he was very gentle, really,' the vet said to my astonishment, and added, 'I've never heard of a cat called Rover.' I thought this was not the time to tell him the tale of the Land Rovers; every extra minute of misery to the Woodpile Cat was a minute of sympathetic distress to me, too. I think I never did tell him, so perhaps he still does not know why the big black cat was called Rover.

Rover forgave us completely and settled into the household in what I can only describe as a state of total confidence. After his long running war with all humanity he made peace with our section of the species, and it was a peace without any distrust. For our part it was disarming and a little disturbing to be believed in so completely, but we have tried with fairness not to betray this trust, while maintaining the more conditional trust that we have always enjoyed from the two Burmese. Sean said that Rover had a security complex, and went on frivolously to account for his state of mind and heart by the suggestion that he may have been thinking himself dead, one of the many guns aimed at him having found its target at last: the fact that he might now be in heaven would explain the change of human attitude towards him. 'We are all angels in his philosophy,' Sean expounded, 'and of course he must be an angel, too: and so you understand his bewilderment when you keep him from your plate at garden meals, because all angels are equal.'

I said there were archangels.

'You don't mean you consider yourself one of them?' my son frankly asked me.

Rover always liked to have a head-rest. On my knee after meals

Rover loved to tear it up

The cubs played like all young things

The tractor lay on its side

Legs Selassie

he would arrange himself so that his head was on the table, however uncomfortable the rest of him might be; or if I were trying to write he would put his heavy head on my arm. I used to imagine him in his woodpile peering out at the hostile world with his chin on a spar of wood, like a sniper at a gun-emplacement. We spoke of making a head-rest for him; some elegant thing of oriental inspiration, carved in hardwood with a waisted stand and shaped top, but there seems never to have been the time and the wood and the skill all together.

One thing that Rover's confidence had yet to achieve was the trust that when we went away from the farm we would surely return. Heaven was clearly made up only of the angels within it. He would follow us to the garage – which was also the heifer-shed and hay-loft – anxiously watching us get into the car and drive away. Whether we were gone for half an hour or half a day or longer, he would be in the garage waiting to receive us. His place was in the hay above the heifers, and as soon as we had switched off the engine we would hear his voice coming nearer as he made his ponderous descent and approached with high waving plume.

'Good dog, Rover!' we would call, gathering parcels, and one could see him purring, his flanks moving in and out, but we could seldom hear this fairly new accomplishment, for when we first made truce with him Rover did not know how to purr. He had had no occasion. Like playing, it was outside his experience. But now it had come to him and he could do it after his fashion; the only thing lacking was the sound effect.

Sometimes at meals he would be sitting behind me on my chair waiting for the signal that eating was finished so that he could come round and settle on my knee. Usually he would start purring and I would feel the pressure exerted at second intervals, with occasional large sighs of sufficient pushing power for me to lose half an inch of chair-room.

We were anxious for Rover's good health in view of the arduous kittenhood he must have experienced, and after the flea-blitz we cleaned and treated his ears, with much pained tolerance on his part, and we introduced him to yeast tablets, which are spurned by both the Burmese. Rover loved them. One might say he doted on them. He would leave even meat for a couple of these; and although he was a slow learner in most things – given to long deliberations – he instantly learned to open and tip the tin if it was placed before him, and greatly enjoyed the game of seeing if he could wolf more than his ration as the tablets poured out, before we could gather up the surplus.

Our wild cat began quickly to acquire many names. From Land Rover to Hey Rover was the first transition, but for a time my husband called him Robert, and not even he seemed to know why. As the hairy one he was often called Esau but this name did not stick; it didn't suit him. One of his most long-lasting names was Fluddles, later contracted to Floods. This did not have the connotations that one might think; it derived from Fluffy-Cuddles, an outrageous pet-name given him by some of the family. Floods becoming one of his regular run of names gave rise to the splendid appellation of Diluvian – not post- or ante- but straight Diluvian; he *was* the Floods; but we found this name difficult to call and it is used now only for formal occasions.

A further name, and one of the favoured ones, came of looking in the dictionary for some quite conventional word (sullage, I think it was) and promptly – as always happens in our family – finding several previously unknown words to beguile us. One of these was *Sumph; a soft sheepish fellow*. Now it may seem strange, in view of what I have told of his history, but since his indoctrination his character had undergone a dramatic change in favour of tolerance and peace (I did remark at the time that there might be something useful to learn from this in the matter of the character of world leaders). Soft and sheepish was pushing the description rather far, but it was done in affection and The Sumph was added to his titles, now and again modified by the suffix 'or sumphing'.

Life with the angels had the effect of reinforcing Rover's confidence to such a degree that he began to break The Rule. Our cats have to submit to virtually only one rule; 'Cats do not get on to the kitchen table.' He seemed to have added a proviso to this; 'Sitting on newspaper is not sitting on the table.' If ever we went out leaving news or other papers on the big table we should certainly come back to find Rover sprawled in the midst of the torn-up remnants. He would not then hasten guiltily to lower levels but would look at us with innocent righteousness; 'As you will see, I am not lying on the table.'

I remember one occasion when all the angels in all the heaven must have been on Sean's side. In some incredible lapse of memory he had gone last and late to bed leaving spread open on the table a hand-drawn map that was part of the project for his first degree. I was the first down the next morning. A mixture of horror and thankfulness swept over me as I saw the map intact upon the table. Rover was curled beside the Aga, and he blinked at me in what seemed a wise and all-knowing way. The map was completely unblemished; there was not so much as a black hair on it; it had not even been sat upon.

Rover greatly enjoyed being swept with the broom in the mornings. Whenever it was fetched from the boiler-room he would galumph across the floor to cast himself down in front of it. I thought this truly remarkable, since it seemed fairly certain that any earlier acquaintance he may have had with brooms was of a menacing nature.

I remember the wonderstruck look on the face of a house-guest once when I took the broom and calling, 'Floods!' swept him with the tiles while adding, 'No cat in all the world is called Floods, except only our Rover. Good dog, Rover!'

My young granddaughter Lindsey wrote a poem to him about this time.

Rover's christian name is Land;
Pretty peculiar and
He is a huge hairy cat,
Take it at that.
Though once quite wild
He is now very mild.
His long hair
Gets difficult to wear.
He looks like a heap of black fur.
His purr is quite a purr.
He is sometimes funny,
And hates being combed on his tummy.
Now he is fatso
Catso.

# CHAPTER TEN

AUGUST that year was a time of very heavy rains; days and nights of rain and cold. It was poor badger-watching weather, but when I could I went out to the Valley, sometimes in the rain. The badgers eventually were forced, I noticed, to take in green bracken for bedding, so sodden was the woodland floor. They would bite through the standing stalks and gather up the fronds, rustling down backwards through the rain with their feathery green bundles tucked under their throats, to disappear – plomp – down into the sett.

The cubs played with all the abandon of young things whatever the weather, whirling about in a maelstrom of thrashing fern-fronds, yikkering excitedly. A cub's coat fluffs out like a dandelion clock when he is really excited, as at playing times, and I would see white puffed-up tails and fluffy bodies bouncing and leaping in the green like a school of small fantasy dolphins, while their elders soberly gathered in the bedding.

I longed to capture some of these scenes on film, but my badger photography was suffering a hiatus. I had almost abandoned my old close-range system, because of its disruption of normal badger life, and had not devised a satisfactory new one. I was now doing most of my watching from the further side of the Valley, looking across the stream. Here on the ledges dug in the valley-side I could sit in comfort – almost luxury after the watching-places I had been used to – with room for friends and cats beside me. It was almost like being in an outdoor theatre; the tiered seats with steps leading up to them, the overhead canopy and, best of all, the quite splendid expanse of stage in its incomparable woodland setting. Watchers on the ledges can command a view of the whole range of Valley badger-setts and the paths connecting them, from the four holes serving the beech-tree complex to the five well-separated main sett entrances and the one distant stream sett hole which can just be seen through hanging foliage. Good large-objective field glasses bring the badgers right up to the viewer's eyes in hair-sharp detail.

With a telephoto lens it would be possible to obtain quite splendid photographs, if the lighting problem could be solved. Even in high summer, when badgers are out well before sunset, the light under the woodland canopy is very dim, and during most of the year they do not emerge before dusk. A telephoto lens would be easy to acquire, once one had decided to spend so large a sum of money, but a tele-flash – that to me, and to my dealers, was an unheard-of thing. Probably such flash-guns were available, at high prices and through specialised channels, but most dealers would not even have known about them. Normal electronic flash in open woodland cannot reach to ranges of 15 metres plus, which was what I needed.

Natalka and I did once try out her telephoto lens, with natural lighting in June when this was at its maximum, and with the largest aperture that would give us any depth of field, but the results were, as we expected, under-exposed.

In any case the rains of that late summer inevitably shelved my problem for me and I contented myself with watching, huddled in a raincoat and sou'wester and listening to the mingled noises of spate-running stream and rain on foliage; the Valley was a water-world, dim-green, wet and shining. It was hard for the tawny owlets squeaking and floating through the branches, struggling to make their always tough way in the world, with the rain blinding their hunting and the blackbirds always mobbing them with loud harsh cries.

Sean and I brought home in a sack three badger-cubs from another part of Surrey. They had been orphaned by the killing of the parents and turned out by the destruction of their sett. Luckily we heard about them in time and were allowed to collect them in their sack from a farmer's woodshed, where they had been for nearly 24 hours. They were too old to attempt taming with any prospect of success, and anyway surely freedom to a wild animal is the supreme need.

We took them to an isolated disused sett in the north woods of the farm and opened the sack at the entrance. The cubs were so chilled and damp and frightened – the sack was wet with their urine – that we had to encourage them to move, but once they started they ran down quickly into the dry darkness. We left food and water near the entrance and raked the sandy earth outside so that it would show tracks. They were just old enough, I thought, to make out on their own, with a little help if needed: we could only hope that the regular Valley badgers would at least not be hostile and at best might enfold them in their clan.

The cubs did not come out at all on the first night, nor during the following day. They did not emerge on the second night during the hours that I was watching, nor did I see them at dawn, but tracks showed that they had been out and had eaten some of the food left for them. From then onwards it became very difficult to be sure what had happened. Certainly they left the sett in which we had introduced them. Two days later a cub of about their size was found dead on the main road, a mile or so away. Looking at the map I saw that the place was in a fairly straight line between our Valley and the cubs' place of origin – some forty miles distant. Do badgers have a homing instinct and was this cub trying to get back? I do not know; I do not even know if it was one of the three orphans.

The other two remained outside my observations for two and a half weeks, and then I made a count of five cubs in the family at the main sett in the Valley, and concluded with joy and I think fair reasonableness that Dorcas had adopted them; and I wished again that I had some system of across-the-stream photography.

Now it was near the end of August, the 27th in fact. I shall never forget that day or that date.

I had felt tired that afternoon and had gone up to read and rest on my bed. Sean was working at his microscope in the kitchen and Bill was in Barn field cutting and carrying grass for silage. I fell asleep, I remember, to the sound of the tractor and forage harvester; and then suddenly Sean was banging on the door, bursting in.

'Ma! Dad's hurt himself. Very badly. He may even be dead.'

I said, 'I'm coming!' and was tumbling out of sleep and across the room and downstairs.

'The tractor turned over. I heard it. I'll go back. Get the ambulance, will you?'

I think it took a few minutes but it seemed hours as desperate emergencies always do – explaining what had happened and where the farm was, clearly and in the fewest possible words – and then making oneself think practically (snatch up something light and warm, and some clean white material) and making one's shaky legs run fast through the house and garden and yard and up Barn field. The red tractor lay on its side with the forage harvester and trailer jack-knifed against it; this was all that I could see as I ran. Sean was kneeling beside it and he came to meet me, his arm round me.

'The tractor rolled right over him; he's clear of it now. He's alive but not really conscious.'

We put the eiderdown over him for warmth; the clean pillow-case across his head where the injuries were bad. I held his hand and Sean talked to him reassuringly. For us – and perhaps for Bill – time came to a stop; but both the police and our own incomparable doctor were with us within fifteen minutes; our doctor had left his surgery patients and come immediately and fast. The ambulance was in the field a few minutes later.

Our doctor – whom I shall call Ted as we always do; he is Amanda's father – persuaded me not to go with the ambulance. I sat with Sean in the wet grass of Barn field and watched the stretcher lifted, and listened to Ted, and realized in numbness that our world, as we had known it for nearly 21 years, was ending. I could be no use at the hospital, Ted told me. I could only sit waiting, perhaps for a long time, while the surgeons and nurses did what they could. Bill would not know me, or whether I was there or not. I must think, too, about the farm. We were without help, in a period between students; the herd must be milked somehow that afternoon and in the days that followed, and calves must be fed and cared for.

The ambulance moved away, bumping gently down the field. We left the police to their investigation and walked back to the farm-house. Here for what seemed a timeless period we three sat in the kitchen. From depths of wisdom Ted understood the character of the situation; the uselessness of words, the need of quiet being-there, and the physical needs, too. Brandy, I heard him suggest, and Sean found the Benedictine. I was grateful for it; I expect we all were.

For a while we were silent. Ted has known always that whatever it might be I wanted the truth, and presently he told us. Bill might not live through the night. He was not sure if there was brain damage, but it was very close.

There was another silence.

He would tell Amanda, he said; he knew she would come back at once.

She did.

Sean had never gone deeply into the study and practicalities of cows and milking, but he knew the general principles. Amanda, like Bill, knew every cow by name and all its idiosyncrasies. I could hear the two of them in the milking-shed as, automatically, I fed the chickens.

'I never saw a cow so cow-hocked; how do you get the clusters on?'

'That's Imogen; you tread on one hoof till she moves it. Dorcas is the tricky one; she stands knock-kneed and pigeon-toed but she's the best milker we've got . . . '

Something terrible happens and life seems almost to go on in the same way, so much that is normal must be done; but really it is all changed, one knows this, and it will never be the same again. Even if he made a complete recovery – and this would take a long time – Bill was not at the age to start farming again after disaster.

In the evening after a supper that nobody wanted we tried to assess the situation. 'Still holding his own,' was all the news the hospital had for us. We could ring again in the morning. We held the inevitable inquiry among ourselves about the accident; how had it happened? The slope was not excessive – much less steep than several on this farm where all of us were accustomed to drive a tractor and implement. The field was wet – it had been raining as usual that month – and this may have been a contributing factor. The forage harvester and trailer had jack-knifed, forcing the tractor over; perhaps the weight of damp grass in the trailer had levered the forage harvester and lifted the weight from the rear wheels of the tractor. The mercy was that the tractor had turned over once more, rolling clear of Bill; the thought of extracting him from under it was intolerable.

'One thing we must do,' Amanda said, 'is find someone else to help with the farmwork and milking. Sean is working for his degree and ought to be free to get on with it, and it's too much for just me.'

Sean said we all knew the cost of relief milkers, and this crisis was going to last for a long time; but Amanda said she knew someone. He was called Joe. He was a metropolitan policeman and luckily he was on sick leave. She knew he would come and be delighted. He would be useful, too; he was a farmer's son and strong and reliable.

I suggested that sick leave wasn't a good state to be in for a Punch

Bowl Farm helper at the moment, but Amanda said it was only Joe's knees; he'd had cartilage trouble, but it wouldn't worry him as he needn't do much walking. He was a marvellous player on the guitar, too – she would fetch hers from home and we could cheer ourselves with songs and music. She would write to him that evening.

# CHAPTER ELEVEN

TELEPHONING in the early morning we were told that although his chance was frail Bill was still holding on. He had multiple injuries but the surgeons had not operated, and probably they would not be able to do so for some days. The hope was that he might slowly gain the strength needed to stand an operation at all. But they were optimistic now about the absence of brain damage, as he had regained consciousness and spoken lucidly for a moment about the circumstances of the accident. He was in the Intensive Care Ward and we could now see him at any time.

The rule was for relations only. Sean and I called for my daughter Shelley at her house in Godalming. In the hospital we were given white gowns and taken to Bill. He was conscious but unable to see or talk to us clearly. It seemed impossible that anyone could be so badly injured and yet survive: he had multiple fractures of the skull and of the right eye-socket, cheek-bone and both jaw-bones; several broken ribs and extensive bruising and laceration; but he knew us and returned our hand-squeeze. I cannot write how we, his family, felt as we looked at his face. Anyone with any heart and imagination will know.

He tried to talk, and we could just make out the words. It was hard to believe it but up came the old dead-pan humour (we had never known whether to take him seriously or not); 'Third time lucky, they say; but I'm getting more practised at it.'

It was true; he had turned the tractor over three times in our life at the farm. Once there had been no one on it; the second time when it broke his arm he had walked down to the farmhouse to tell us.

We did what we could to reassure him about the farm.

'Amanda and I are milking,' Sean said. 'Everything's O.K.'

Bill tried to give us some vital information or advice but we couldn't understand it. 'We'll find out soon enough,' Sean said as we were ushered from the ward. 'About Shannon, probably – the fastest hoof on the farm. Remember Jill's nosebleed?'

Whatever the advice was, often we needed it, and more besides. Suddenly there were just the three of us to do and think of everything, making decisions without Bill while desperately worrying about him. Were the cows to graze Upper Six Acres or would he be relying on us to cut it for silage? How could we cut it, or do any field work, without the tractor? How long would it take to get the tractor repaired, and ought we to hire one?

To help with any inquiry Sean took photographs of the accident scene before the tractor and implements were towed away. Bill too would be certain to want to study them to see what really had happened, we told ourselves, believing against all odds in his recovery.

Joe telephoned in the morning with a Scottish voice. He had just had Amanda's letter and would arrive early in the evening. He couldn't bring his guitar because someone else had it ('Everything belongs to everyone in our London set,' Amanda told me) but they could both use Amanda's, he said.

He proved to be huge and kind, and witty in the dry way that we were used to from Bill. His father was a beef farmer; he had no experience of dairy but guessed he'd get the hang of it. We were not to thank him; frankly he was glad to be out of London for a bit while his knees were running-in again.

Amanda now revealed that she also was on a kind of sick leave with an obstinate infected cut under her foot. We all knew that I had a groggy wrist since breaking a small bone in it earlier that summer. 'What a gang of crocks we are!' she said cheerfully. 'One bad foot, two bad knees and a groggy wrist.'

No one seemed to make any concessions about it. Amanda tip-toed about like someone in a modern ballet using gumboots; Joe audibly creaked and I dropped things, but we got through. For a time Sean commuted between his microscope and the milking-clusters but after a few days Joe was on top of the job enough for Amanda and him to manage.

Each day I was at the hospital, sometimes alone but often with Sean and Shelley and even Amanda, who was as much family as anyone by all reasonable logic. There was little change in Bill. For a few days he seemed to hover on the edge of life, scarcely aware of us or of anything else, connected to blood and plasma bottles and fed by tube. There were no specific visiting hours in this ward. I sat there – mostly in silence; I think he was comforted by mere presence – for hours each day. One or other of the nurses was with him every five minutes; nothing that could be done for him was not done.

Sometimes he drifted up from half-consciousness and recognized one of us, his fingers tightening on the hand holding his hand, or murmuring something that we would try to understand, leaning close to him.

I think that he did just hold his own; any gain in strength, enough for a big operation, seemed imperceptible. Throughout these days we were told, and I think we knew, that he might die at any time. But still his doctors insisted that there was an improvement, and still they hoped and expected to operate on the fifth day if his improvement were maintained.

I found myself completely unable to work at writing, and I worried about it because of the approaching deadline I had set myself for my book, *A Wind is Blowing*.

'You know you won't be able to write until after the operation,' Sean told me. 'How about taking on the temporary job of Mosser's Mate?'

Released now from the cowshed he was back at his survey of the ecology of wet heathland, with special reference to the distribution of sphagnum species. For much of each day with instruments and notebook he was working on the bog at Elstead, three miles away from the farm. Gumboots he considered a nuisance, filling up with water and hampering movement; he believed in canvas running shoes and leaving his jeans to dry on him between sessions. Feeling middle-aged and old-fashioned I raised the subject of paving the way for later rheumatism and naturally was grinned at.

I of course wore wellingtons and tried to keep the water out. I shall always remember one occasion when, floundering and sinking below their rims I saw Sean turn and look at me with mock anxiety. 'Shall I take the notebook?'

On the fifth day after the accident Bill's doctors conferred in the morning. There was a serious risk in operating but the risk might be greater in waiting longer. They decided against waiting. In the afternoon Bill underwent the first and longest of a series of operations. We knew that he might not survive it, but he did. I think that his nurses were nearly as delighted as we were when they took us to him the next day, and the old dry humour came up scarcely audible through bandages and padding. 'Must be – indestructible. How's – the tractor?'

During the following weeks Bill's hold on life strengthened, so that even from day to day we could see the difference. Except for one terrifying set-back when infection got into his crushed ear and endangered his brain, his improvement was steady and often astonishing.

At his request we brought baskets of luscious fruits. Still on tube feeding he could not eat them, but he wanted to give them to his nurses. His shelves were crowded every day with cards and letters which he could not read. We would take them down and read them to him; the nurses had already done this but he liked to hear them again. Amanda and Sean who both have special talent in this line added cards of their own painting, usually hilarious scenes of cowshed life which amused the nurses. These originals seem unfortunately to have disappeared with the tide of events, but I have salvaged a pleasing doodle from the telephone pad. I think that Amanda drew it and Sean added the captions.

With Joe in the household our burden was greatly lightened. As well as bringing a general unruffled efficiency he was such fun to have around; and we needed cheerfulness – it was easy suddenly to be on the edge of tears or near to shouting at someone for almost nothing at all.

A true Scot, Joe was enchanted with our porridge. All our lives together Bill and I have made real oatmeal porridge, and he can make it as well as I do. It scarcely takes two minutes on the Aga at night and is ready to eat in the morning.

In Scotland, the land of porridge, it is revered and served with ceremony. Spoken of in the plural as 'Them', it is eaten standing, so I have been told; Joe and I could not agree as to whether this is done out of respect or to allow room for greater intake. We plunged into the usual arguments about sugar versus salt or neither, and whether it was proper to use a spoon or a spurtle. Sometimes I suggested to him that it was 'Them' which kept him with us, but I knew it was his kindness of heart.

In the evenings after the day's farm-work, bog-hopping and

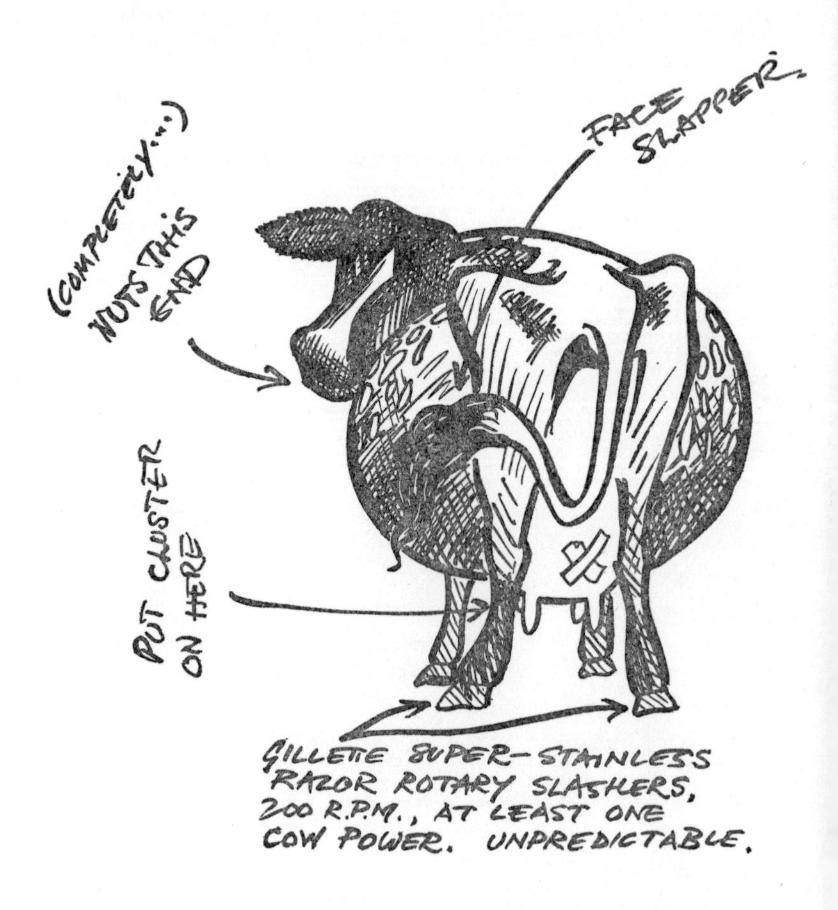


hospital visiting we would have 'folk' sessions in the warm kitchen: Amanda sitting with one foot in a saucer of formaline solution as she played and sang to her guitar; Sean with one eye at his microscope, the table half-covered with sphagnum species, and I writing letters. Joe would listen critically, tapping a foot, before reaching to snatch the guitar. 'No! It goes like this.'

Sometimes I had to tell them not to play such heart-breaking songs, and they would burst into joyful jigs and ditties, the guitar changing hands so that I never knew whether to expect the music from my right side or my left. I liked best of all Amanda's own songs, which I considered far superior to much that was being broadcast at the time.

Her brother Charles turned up one morning when I was at the hospital. He brought a superb whisky fruit cake that he had baked himself and cleaned the farmhouse kitchen and went home. Our friend Hugh Blackburne came over from his own farm and sorted out our electric fence and other problems; so many people came and supported and cheered us. I remember it all with appreciation; it meant much to me then.

The herd flourished in Joe's and Amanda's care, the milk yield scarcely going down at all under the unfamiliar management; but we knew that this arrangement must be temporary, that we were only postponing the big problem – what was to be done about the herd? Bill was making incredible progress, when one considered the extent of his injuries, but he was still on the danger list. It might be months before he would be out of hospital. In two or three weeks Sean would be back at university; Amanda's and Joe's sick leave would have ended and I should be alone at the farm.

I saw ahead of me, like a looming mountain that almost certainly cannot be avoided, the sale of the herd that had taken us more than twenty years to establish. It seemed at first unthinkable even to mention this matter to Bill. I think we hoped that he might mention it himself, but all talking was difficult and was kept to a minimum. The longer the matter was left, the less time there would be for a sale to be catalogued and advertised. Eventually we decided to ask our agent to prepare for a sale in early October, while understanding that we might have to cancel it at the last minute if we were not able to receive Bill's approval.

It was sad work, the cataloguing in their families of these animals which were known so well to us; almost like arranging for the sale of one's friends and relations.

Bill's approval came in time for the sale to be conducted on the agreed date – the day before my three helpers were to leave. We should dispose of the herd, he said, but keep two for our own use; a single cow is a lonely unhappy creature.

It might seem an impossible thing to decide which two from a herd of homebred cattle should stay behind, and at first it was so. There was Nerissa, one of the really good Shakespeare cows; Rose of Tralee, the last daughter of Shelley's favourite, Duchess; Lorelei, daughter of Rhinegold; the beautiful Redwood; Dorcas, whom Bill considered the best we had ever bred; Imke and Jane and Lindsey and Amanda, who were named for special people.

In the end, as so often happens, the choice seemed to be made of its own accord. For two people and occasional extras we did not need a high-yielding cow. We ought not to keep one good enough to fetch a high price at the sale – and this meant eliminating any recently calved. We needed a cow likely to be amenable to hand-milking and placid enough to accept the loss of nearly all her familiar companions.

There was only one animal which fulfilled all these requirements. This was Dewdrop – Punchbowl Oxford Dewdrop – on whom children rode and cats jumped and people leaned in conversation. Not due to calve until February she was still giving more than enough milk for our needs. And to keep her company which heifer could Amanda and I possibly choose but Trellis, the orphan we had reared in the kitchen? Just over a year old now, she might be expected to come into milk as Dewdrop was drying off at the end of the next summer.

I looked up out of the window at the herd coming down to the milking and tried to imagine the yard with two cows waiting.

Slow return to health and strength: Bill and the author

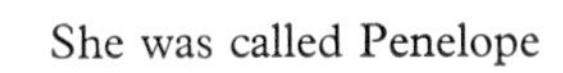

She was called Penelope

The mother would take her cub and drag it to safety

# CHAPTER TWELVE

'THE unexpected dispersal of this fine herd of prize-winning pedigree and purebred dehorned Jerseys,' the catalogue said. 'Nothing has been purchased for the last ten years. The herd has always been entirely disease free . . . '

I found it hardly bearable to see them go, each with a lot-number pasted on her rump, walking round the strawed sale ring at our garden gate – Gossamer, Shantung, Starfish, Spindrift, Moonshine, Macushla, Lace . . . one after another the wrenches came. Each one I had known as a calf and heifer; most of them I had named, some I had bottle-fed; their dams and granddams were known to me.

Dewdrop and Trellis too were at the sale, bought-in for us by the auctioneers as the custom is.

Copper stood watching mystified over the Orchard gate, his heifer companions gone away from him. There had been little time for riding him lately, little time for anything but the hospital and keeping the farm going. I thought about Copper now, to keep my heart from aching as the auctioneer's voice called the names and particulars. Copper would be lonely. Young heifers had been able to share the sparser grazing which a pony must have if he is not to get soft and fat, but a milking cow must have richer fare. Copper could not have Trellis, who was to be Dewdrop's companion. I must think of something else for him – a donkey, perhaps – when I had time to think at all . . .

Shannon, Juliet, Silk, Tiffany, Tussore; the herd was passing out of our lives . . . I supposed that still there were badgers in the Wild Valley, but for weeks I had not been down there. On this evening not only would the herd be gone, but my helpers too would all be away and for the first time since we came here I should be alone on the farm. Perhaps I would slip down to the woods and see the badgers.

In the evening I was too busy clearing up but in the night I did go to the woods, and in what now seem to me rather ridiculous circumstances. For the first time since early childhood I woke up suddenly afraid in the silent lonely house, imagining I had heard footfalls, and was overcome by the urge to escape. Moving in the dark so that a light should not draw attention to me I reached for jeans and jersey and, as so often for more trivial reasons, made a streak for the woods. This was my place; here I felt safe. Wild animals never frightened me: the only times when I have been uneasy in the woods were when I detected human presence near me.

Now in the starlit Valley I felt calmer, amused at myself, and yet in some way at peace with the things that were happening to me, to us all, to our life and possibly our home. The woods were so quiet, so changeless, the tall beeches lifting as they always had, the only sound from their leaves and the running stream. But there was another sound, a quick trotting through the leaf-litter, fast approaching.

I stood where I was, still against a beech-trunk, and there crossing the grassy track before me were five badgers in the starlight – Dorcas, her mate and their three cubs. It was five weeks since I had seen them.

I watched the pale dumpy tails bustling into deeper shadow, and for a short time heard the gusty crunchings of beech and hazel nuts; then quietness settled on the woods again and I walked home comforted and reassured. It did not surprise me to find no trace of any intruder; all was as usual and the cats, asleep beside the Aga, opened wondering eyes to look at me as I padded through the kitchen.

All the same, for the rest of my nights alone in the house I took to bed with me a .410 shotgun loaded with blank cartridges. At least if I were frightened again I could fire it out of the window into the sky and make a – to me – comforting noise.

I never had occasion to fire it. This was probably because I was much too tired and sleepy to imagine things again in my solitary weeks at the farm.

Trouble met me at the start in Dewdrop's objecting to hand-milking. This really surprised me; our docile riding-cow, who would follow one like a well-trained dog and allow children to garland her neck, who mothered other cows' calves and was kind to cats and hens and strangers, sweeping aside my bucket with an uncompromising hind-leg veto. It was of course many years since we had milked by hand: our whole herd was accustomed only to the machine; but everyone knew that one could do anything with Dewdrop and that was why we had kept her. We had been wrong – I, at least, could not convert her in the matter of milking. Subjected to her pitying looks and ruthless footwork I tried every ruse that I had ever heard of, while Trellis watched interested through the doorway.

Finally, in total defeat, I went to the quite ridiculous length of rigging up a single unit to the four-cow milking machine and milking her in the manner to which she was accustomed. With my unmechanical approach this system involved placing a large Aga pan (for the milk) on a block of wood on an empty detergent drum (to get the right height) and fixing the suction-lid of the in-churn unit to the top of the pan, which was flat enough to allow a proper seal in a way impossible with a bucket – I was not of course going to use a whole ten-gallon churn for which the system was designed.

So far so good, as they say, but now I was in trouble with regulating the pulsator, which was too fast. It should I knew run at about one pulse per second, but how to adjust the regulator was a mystery beyond my simple understanding. Dewdrop and I came to some kind of mistrustful armistice about it, mixed with contempt on her part, until Sean managed to get down for a week-end and put it right in a matter of moments. 'You've got milk in the air-pipes, too: and don't you need a fresh lot of caustic? It's just as well I did come down.'

The problem of Copper's loneliness blew up almost immediately. The day after the sale I had gone to the hospital leaving him in the field called Hanger (referring to 'hanging woods', on a steep slope), while Dewdrop and Trellis were in Barn field handy for milking. All seemed at peace as I drove away, and I had a splendid afternoon with Bill who, maintaining his wonderful progress, could eat ice cream (after a fashion and very independently, refusing any help – 'I can manage the spoon myself') as he listened to my carefully edited accounts of farm life.

Coming home in the late afternoon, thinking about the pulsator, all seemed fairly normal as I drove into the garage. A small huddle of fans stood by the garden gate (all authors have them) and I said that they could take a photograph of the farmhouse if they liked but I was rather busy, and that moment my eyes took in the incredible sight of Dewdrop and Trellis careering down Barn field like the Thundering Herd with, unbelievably, Copper at full gallop in pursuit.

Ahead of them was a barbed wire fence shutting off the Little Orchard; they would have to stop there, I thought, running into the yard. Dewdrop was far gone in calf and very big – she was at the best of times a low-slung cow with a heavy udder – and I feared for her after such a gallop; but rounding the corner of the barn I saw a further quite incredible thing. Hippo-sized and hippo-shaped Dewdrop was flying through the air, taking the wire fence like a National Hunt chaser with little Trellis half a length behind. Copper at her tail – the only one of the three who might conceivably have been expected to perform such a jumping feat – astonishingly dug in his toes and slithered to a stop.

I left him champing up and down the fence while I tore back to intercept Dewdrop, fearing at least a badly torn udder and at worst a dead calf before nightfall.

Wildly excited after their exploits Dewdrop and Trellis had bucked their way down the Orchard and barged through the wicket-gate to finish on the forecourt, where they were fiercely goring the straw-bales left over from the sale.

I hurried to put a halter on Dewdrop and to inspect the barbed-wire damage, the bunch of fans calmly looking on as though nothing out of the way were happening. The third incredible thing then came home to my battered intelligence: no visible damage at all had been sustained to Dewdrop's udder or the rest of her anatomy; there was not a scratch, not even to her hind-legs following last and lowest. She had cleared the fence cleanly, a faultless jump and deserving of award. She did not receive one, I am sorry to admit. After a cursory examination of Trellis I raced back with the halter to attempt the capture of Copper, who was by now tearing the air with his screaming snorts and the turf with his hoofs.

This task took some time and much strategy, as he was by now in a fairly wild state. When eventually I got the halter on him and swinging in circles was leading him from the field with my one good hand, I saw the fans leaning on the wall still peacefully watching: and then of course I realized – conditioned by my tales of high adventure they *did* think that this was perfectly normal Punchbowl Farm life.

When after much search I had found the small gap in Copper's hedge it took me a long time, with my left hand only, to repair it enough to last until Sean was back at the week-end; two things already on my helpless-female list for him, the fence and the pulsator – I did not know then about the milk in the air-pipes.

One thing I did now know; I must get a companion for Copper pretty quickly. The same evening, on the telephone to our friends the Blackburnes, it was arranged for me to receive as field-guests a donkey-mare named Josephine and her foal Alice, both used to ponies and of a phlegmatic disposition.

In the matter of Dewdrop the angels must all have been in my favour because, against any normal odds, she did not lose her calf. There she was early in the morning as usual, waiting with Trellis for me to come and make my pitiful attempts to milk her, sighing deeply as I fumbled with the Aga pan and wood-block. She looked sidelong down her flanks at me in a commiserating way that was almost totally humbling and then settled herself to chew resignedly while the inept performance proceeded.

The donkeys arrived alone in a very large cattle-truck. We put them in the little paddock on the other side of the drive from Copper's field, so that when he came over the hill of Hanger and saw them acquaintance could begin with the safety of two fences and the drive between them. Josephine was small, black, prim and very reserved. Baby Alice, shy and looking just like a doormat, went round behind Mum and peeped mistrustfully over her back at me.

Quite quickly Copper got wind of the visitors and came pounding over the hill with his mane and tail flying. I stood my ground on the drive and felt like Horatius, prepared to be felled in the onslaught, but my drama fizzled out. Copper was enchanted, fascinated, grateful and anxious; he wanted to make sure that these delectable creatures would not now be taken from him and he trotted archly up and down the fence, whinnying and whuffling ingratiatingly.

The donkeys took practically no notice at all, except that Josephine nosed her child further out of sight behind her, as one who might say, 'We are not going to speak to that nasty stranger, are we!'

Disappointed and crestfallen Copper hung about the fence for the rest of the morning; at least he was there when I returned from the hospital at noon. He looked at me in the manner of a dog who has not been taken for his usual walk, hope still present but diminishing.

I opened the gates and led Josephine and Alice to join him. Overjoyed by this good fortune Copper must have thought that the ladies had come across to him of their own accord, and immediately suggested a little gallop all together: but Josephine put on her hard-to-get act. Disapproving and distant she took her child aside to graze in a place apart. So tiny and toylike was Alice that she only needed four wheels and a handle.

# CHAPTER THIRTEEN

WHEN Sean had corrected the pulsator and my other troubles in the milking-parlour my sessions down there were so easy as almost to be pleasurable. There was time now to lean on the door-post while the milking peacefully proceeded, talking to Trellis or gazing at the old stone house with its triple yew tree, the scene of so many of my stories.

Dewdrop now accepted me as a kind of well meaning but ineffectual eccentric. I think she held against me the loss of her many companions, and for a long time only tolerated Trellis, who was not of her age-group.

Although at this late stage of her lactation Dewdrop's yield was low, it was more than I and the cats could manage; so once again I started butter-making, as I had done in the pioneer years at the farm before we became commercial dairy farmers. In a small way this was quite profitable, as was my sale of dark-brown free-range eggs: there is a considerable demand even at high prices for food with real flavour, in this age of factory farming.

In the hospital Bill too, now that he was off tube-feeding, was beginning to notice a lack of flavour. This must have been due partly to the paralysis which affected half of his face, but all the same, everything he asked for I brought him (and was allowed to bring him), from Bristol Cream to farm porridge. In this last I think I must have set up a record, for never have I heard of anyone else taking porridge to a patient in hospital. This admirable hospital did make porridge, of course, but it was not 'Them', and no one would have honoured it by standing. In the farm kitchen I made porridge every day for Bill and took it to him in a vacuum jar with farm milk and brown sugar in separate containers.

It was heart-breaking to see how thin Bill was, his back-bone standing out in a ridge. This was the result of long desperate crisis:

everyone was trying to get weight back on him now, and slowly he was responding.

I was getting used to my lonely life at the farm and thought little any more about attackers in the night; but I still kept the shotgun by my bed and once I nearly fired it. The time was after eleven. As I had to be up early I was in bed but not asleep when I heard footsteps approach and then stop on the stone path below my window. A murmured consultation drifted to my ears. Tense with fright I grasped the gun and looked out of the window. Three faces looked up at me in half-moonlight and a voice said a little nervously, 'Please may we camp where we did last year?'

We were well into autumn but the weather was glorious – gold and mellow. I had no real idea who they were, but gladly gave my permission and went thankfully back to bed.

For a week after the donkeys' arrival there was no time to ride Copper, and I was glad to see him content with their company. Josephine remained stand-offish always, but somehow Copper managed to 'adopt' Alice, and generally when I went to see if all were well with them I would find those two together, Alice close to Copper's side while Josephine kept herself at a distance.

Copper was quickly getting fat again. There was thick grass everywhere on the farm now that there was no herd to graze it. This was useful to me in the misty early mornings when I set off through the fields in search of my two cows. Unable in the soft white mist to see clearly across the width of a field, I used now to look for the dark swath of their path through the dew and follow that. Ankle deep, the lush grass squeaked as I brushed through it, my gumboots shining wet and gathering ornaments of small petals, purple grass-seed and curled leaves.

Sometimes as I walked this silent misty world I would come on another solitary walker, Mr Watkins, out with his gun to get a rabbit for his lunch. Always up by six o'clock he would be out in all weathers, his well-worn country clothes nearly invisible against field and woodland background. 'Lovely morning!' I remember him once saying, smiling his real pleasure in it as we paused companionably in enclosing drizzle; and it was lovely, in its own subtle way – soft and warm, like pearl-grey velvet, a private world with no sight or sound or smell of the industrial age that is our sad inheritance.

Presently the comfortable shapes of Dewdrop and Trellis would take form in the pearly-greyness, lying snug against a hedge where their own bodies had kept the dampness from their beds. They would view me with a lack of rapture that was more damping than the mist, waiting until I had prodded them with be-petalled boot before, sighing resignedly, they would rise and stretch and leisurely step homewards.

On bright dry mornings all the cats would come to fetch the cows with me. Hula was the best cow-cat, trotting eagerly over considerable distances, carrying her head high and forging through the deeper grass as one swimming through green water afloat with scabious and clover. Pardos would often fall out from the longer expeditions and wait for her, hidden in some hedge, to jump out and greet her, trilling lovingly, on our return.

Such hours were absorbed by these dawn search-parties, idyllic though they were in all but frightful weather, that I decided once more to restrict the range of my little herd and keep them to Barn field. There was more than ample feed for them there, even allowing for the lower value of autumn grass, and the round-up time was cut by at least two-thirds.

Now at last, straightening my daily problems, I began to see time available for riding again; but after his long lotus-eating with the donkeys Copper was even less inclined than the morning cows to welcome me. When he realized that the donkeys were not coming too he was totally opposed to the idea and did his best to block all my intentions. It was murder getting him past my neighbour's two geese which looked at him from her garden, it was worse forcing him past a peaceful tractor in Sandy Lane. It was quite a ride down to Keeper's Cottage, with no saddle and my gumboots dangling and he behaving like an unbroken colt, neighing back to the donkeys and swinging about the lane in a way that found out one's long unpractised thigh-muscles.

I always rode him unshod about these fields and peat-tracks, and the patter of his hoofs pleased me as he danced about. I also felt quite a sporting old lady when, encountering wondering ramblers, he put on his ferocious stallion act and reared and snorted.

Preoccupied as I was with him it was still possible to appreciate the glorious leaf and bracken colour of late October; but it would grow richer as the year moved into November.

Mr Watkins was not at home, so there were no pear-drops and

no reasons to linger. Copper was away with a leap that would have spanned a fair-sized ditch and heading homewards. All would be lost, I knew, if once he really got out of control: with one wrist and no saddle and a snaffle bridle I could only be a classic brinklady. All the way back up the Wagon Track he tittuped and bucked and shook his head and snorted, heralding with shuddering screams his return to the donkeys. Once he was up on the home fields I knew that I should not be able to hold him and we should probably break both our necks over the silo bank, so at the gate I dismounted and led him. This was almost worse than riding as he was now within braying distance of the donkeys and mad to get back to them before some heartless person took them away again.

My horrified cows saw him coming, and I prayed for peace. Heaven was still in my favour; there was no interest in chasing cows when one's personal donkeys were loudly waiting for one, and we got home without disaster.

More things I learned; I must have a saddle and I must ride Copper much more frequently. Further, I would fit a dropped noseband to the bridle and give my wrist the care it must have if it were to last through my Horatius period.

The Horatius period was much shorter, in fact, than all of us expected. Our highest hope had been that Bill might be home for Christmas, but even this of course was not assured. In the event he left hospital some weeks earlier. His recovery from the first big operation surprised both his doctors and ourselves, and after a period at a convalescent hospital he was allowed to come home to build up his strength for the next in the series.

The times of my real anxieties began.

I need not have been lulled by his extreme caution as I drove him home, requesting a 25 m.p.h. maximum and gripping his seat. I should have known that in a very short time his reckless nature would seek a crack and burst out.

For a few days, and a few days only, he groped his way around the house, seeing with his one eye in focus and hearing with his one undamaged ear. Then came his first short walk, into Yew Tree field, which with dogged independence he insisted on doing alone. I found him there a little later, looking over his bee-hives and tools.

Presently he went down to the milking shed to inspect my arrangements and improve them, and in a few more days he was talking about what he would do when the tractor came back and I found him telephoning the agricultural centre to ask them to be quicker with the repair. My heart dived. It was too much. I said that if he drove the tractor again, with one eye and one ear, I would pack up. It was all very well for him to smash himself but I had to gather up the wreckage.

He took no notice of me. He knew, and I knew, that as soon as the tractor returned he would drive it, and that these were the only terms on which life was any use to him. I should have to learn not only to live with the new anxieties but to give them up. One cannot spend one's days in fear and apprehension: presently acceptance of danger has to be learned, for oneself and one's people, or life is not tolerable at all.

The one thing his doctors did want him to do – daily walking – he did not care about and he managed to resist most of my efforts to persuade him. I recall one walk only, that could really be called a walk. It was on the last day of perfect weather; soft and sunny, and still the coloured trees and bracken lingered in the Valley and the Punch Bowl. We decided to go down the Wagon Track and visit Mr Watkins – too far for the cats but Pardos and Hula appeared from nowhere and joined us. I ran back with them both and put them in the kitchen, with a pair of wellingtons to block the cat-door.

We had not gone much further when, looking up from their grazing, Dewdrop and Trellis saw where we were going and fell in behind. It was many weeks since with the herd they had been down to the Punch Bowl fields, a place much loved by all our cattle.

'Well, why not?' Bill said, and we left the gate open behind us as we turned from the fields into the Wagon Track.

Down here the colour was spectacular – gold and yellow and brown and red and russet, surging up at one side and tumbling down at the other with purest blue between. To see any other person on this road is what a German friend would call 'a very seldom thing', but round a bluff of high copper bracken we encountered Ted, our doctor, and his dog Pip. Free of motor-roads and time-pressure on his day off he was walking out to see Bill. He must have been surprised to meet us both with the cows at heel and so far from home. The sensible thing was to turn round and accompany us to Keeper's Cottage, and this he did, with Dewdrop bucking at Pip all the way down.

Mr Watkins too was surprised, to find three visitors with two cows and a dog at his garden gate, but after we had let Dewy and Trellis into Keeper's field we were all welcomed indoors and sat there in the warm kitchen looking out through the open door, talking of badgers and foxes and deer, and how Copper had broken the gatepost, and how Mr Watkins missed the herd.

When presently she thought we had idled there long enough, Dewdrop jumped her way over the bar followed by Trellis, and we saw through the door the two of them making back along the track. Perhaps they had expected to find the lost herd down there in the Bowl fields, and now disappointed were heading for home.

'They think they can jump anything, after the barbed-wire,' I nearly said, but stopped myself in time: I had not told Bill about this.

'They know their way home,' he said calmly.

# CHAPTER FOURTEEN

ALTHOUGH Bill was maintaining his good progress, sometimes it seemed a long and weary battle for him. It was a winter of constant hospital visits – to Guildford, Haslemere and London for different treatments and tests. Through all this winter and for much longer he was able to see properly with only the one sound eye and hear with one ear, and yet as soon as the tractor returned he was driving it. I had tried to persuade him to sell it before it did return, but I only heard again the tale of how after an accident one must always drive or ride or fly the thing that caused it, and at the earliest moment, or one's nerve would be gone for ever. I said we had to think about my nerve as well, but Bill thought that the same therapy should apply here.

Daily now he would be out and cruising around on this monster – his interpretation, I imagined, of his doctors' orders that he was to go for a good walk every day. I would catch myself half-listening, as I wrote or cooked or gardened, for the sudden change in engine-note; but it was not for me to ordain what he should do with his life. He had never tried to ordain what I did with mine; yet perhaps he too thought that often I was foolish, going alone to the woods at night or even riding a scatty pony bareback, with donkeys loose at heel.

I was riding much oftener now (with saddle and dropped nose-band after the new year) and Copper was settling down quite sensibly. He still made such a great fuss on leaving his donkeys behind that sometimes I let them follow, but this slowed our pace most tediously as he would not outstrip their gentle tripping trot.

That winter a further blow struck our little farm. In February, five weeks after calving, Dewdrop died suddenly of hypomag-nesaemia. There had been no warning; she had seemed absolutely herself a few hours before. This is a mysterious disease which we had never encountered before: it can occur where the incidence of magnesia is normal in the soil.

Not only was this the sad loss of a family pet – our much loved Dewy – it was half our herd gone at a single stroke; it was all our milk supply as well as the milk for her own calf and one we had bought to take the surplus from her bounty; it was Trellis's only companion.

The calves of course had to be sold, and went to the Blackburnes. Now often I had Trellis too behind me when I went riding. It seemed a strange ghost of the old farm – so busy always with cows and calves and field-work and whistling student and shouting Bill – as I rode its silent empty fields on those winter afternoons and thought about the old years.

In that February we acquired an Abyssinian kitten. I had ordered him many months before and forgotten about it because of the things that had happened, but now with pleasure I arranged to collect him. He seemed to us exceptionally beautiful, but in a subtle way, a contrast to the dramatic lines and markings of a Siamese. Puma-like, lynx-like, with honey-fawn ticked coat and lissom movement, he had very unusual dark markings. Just above each hind paw, to the outside rear, he had a black 'thumbprint', very stylish and noticeable as he walked. Round his creamy throat was an elegant dark necklace swung low on his breast and looking as if it should have borne an amulet. A dark thin line ran down his back and along his tail, emphasizing the litheness of his shape. His large delicately tufted ears and copper-amber-gold eyes completed the wildness of his appearance, and if anything further were needed to recommend him to me, his total independence – the spirit to call no man master – would have done so.

We called him Haile Selassie, but this only after extensive and fruitless searches into Ethiopian history and language – both rather depressing. As with all our cats his given name quickly acquired variations and diminutives, the most lasting of which was Legs, conferred to celebrate the elegance of his long limbs. Legs Selassie he became for all daily communications.

He had been graciously received by Rover who, probably still thinking he was in heaven, might have supposed our house to be a place where all animals had a right to be and were welcome. The

Burmese were so forbidding that I thought it best to share my room with Haile for the first few nights, when no one would be at hand downstairs to keep the peace. I made up a bed for him in a box near the radiator and he settled there willingly enough: but quite early he found out the advantages of the continental quilts which our family uses – nothing tucked in – and began a nightly policy of infiltration. I might not have discovered his presence for a time, since he was peaceful and relaxed in repose, except for the six-cylinder purr he would generate as soon as he was under the quilt: it was rather like being in an aeroplane on a night flight to – well, Ethiopia? If he or I turned over, the stilled engines would come on again, roaring soft in the middle of the night.

In those early days Hula was the most hostile of the cats towards him, but she did on one occasion bring him a mouse, probably recognizing her position as hunter to the kittens, for she had hunted for many of her own.

From the beginning he showed himself to be an intelligent and individual kitten. After a few days he mastered the cat-door and in both directions, without ever having been taught. We never saw him experimenting in any way, just going in and out.

When still too young to hunt for himself he would take over relics from Hula's trophies; a rabbit-paw or scut, or a fragment of fur, or a whole unwanted vole. During lulls between games with these toys he liked to hide them in secret places, but often he would forget them. We might at any time come on one or more inside a shoe, in a vacant hole in the egg-rack, behind the central heating pipes and, once, in Sean's handgrip waiting unzipped for last minute additions before the dash for the train. The place most favoured by him and least by us was under the kitchen rugs. He was adept at lifting the edge and pushing his treasure beneath, usually without leaving much obvious bump even over a vole, so that people walked unaware over them. The flattened remains – which became known as his pressed collection – might not be found until kitchen-cleaning day when the rugs were taken up for shaking.

He realized at once that his true ally and friend was Rover, and slept close to him in safety by the Aga. Often when Rover's black fox-brush tail was not covering Rover's nose Haile would be lying stretched along it as on a sumptuous bed, and Rover would tolerate this liberty in the large accepting way that now seemed natural to him. It was difficult to remember our Woodpile Cat in his old role of terrifying despot.

During the winter of Bill's slow return to health and strength I tried not to think too much about our future. I had begun again in a slow desultory way on my long abandoned book, *A Wind is Blowing*. For some months I had felt incapable of writing – at least of writing in any way professionally. Certainly I did not want to write, and I put away every thought of it with repugnance. My publishers were patient and understanding and did not hurry me; but there was no escape from the hard facts of high expenses and dwindling income. We were living on our savings. The farm income had stopped with the sale of the herd, and it transpired that Bill had no personal accident insurance – for every helper on the farm, yes, but not for himself. I saw that I must overcome somehow my aversion and start writing again, but it was a slow and almost agonizing effort of will, made harder by the feeling that no book written under such conditions could hope to be good. That it did in the end receive good notices remains to me one of life's mysteries.

As to the farm itself: I knew that however miraculous Bill's recovery it would not be possible for him at his age to start again and pick up out of the wreckage the arduous life of a working farmer, with the help only of an inexperienced and annually changing student. We had no cottage for a skilled worker, and our application to build one was turned down by the County Council on the grounds of insufficient acreage.

Now we began what was to be a long and disheartening endeavour to solve our problem, without what seemed the inevitability of having to leave the place we had loved and worked in for more than twenty years. Twice we nearly sold the land alone, which would have left us the old house to live in, but on each occasion the prospective buyer found at the last minute some land nearer to his own holding. Other ideas and propositions we considered, including two involving ex-farm students, but always the difficulties were too great to resolve, especially that of accommodation: we were not even successful with an application to use a residential caravan.

With sadness of heart I saw ahead like an approaching doom the sale of all that was home: not only of the fields that we had cleared and made into green pasture, not only of the old house that we had

I cannot imagine how I got on without Frances

There was always delight in seeing the cubs

Hunting out raisins and peanuts

We had real snow at the end of winter

repaired and restored, but of the Wild Valley, with its deer and badgers and foxes, my perfect place and my refuge.

But still we did not put the farm on the market – miracles do seem sometimes to happen – and now when I rode Copper in the woods and fields of early spring, I saw all this lovely land with a sharpened awareness.

# CHAPTER FIFTEEN

EARLY that spring Josephine went home to have her new foal, and her ex-baby Alice departed in the back of a car with a family who had just bought her: but Copper was not left desolate. A new donkey came at once to keep him company. She was as different from Josephine as a donkey could be – white and big where she was black and small; friendly and confiding, even pushful, where she had been remote – but Copper loved her from the start.

She was called Penelope – we seemed fated to have polysyllabic donkeys – and she wore a traditional dark cross upon her spine. A very inquisitive – one might say nosy – donkey, she required to share in all the doings around her. At once I foresaw an intensified programme of riding with a donkey at heel – indeed of feeding hens, cutting nettles, pruning fruit trees and just sitting in the sun with a donkey in attendance, and so it was to be.

Activities in which she could not join distressed and annoyed her. Rolling was one of these. Several times I saw her watching Copper indulge in this exercise when we came in from riding; he was the perfect shape for it, plump and roly-poly. His little unshod hoofs would wave luxuriously in the air as he went over and over, wriggling his back in the grass to get rid of the feel of the saddle; and she would watch with anxious concentration as one who yearns to master a skill but finds it elusive. Presently down she would go, heaving her thin white legs off the ground but seldom achieving the ultimate swing over; for unlike Copper, Penelope was not the shape for rolling, her high withers and spine making finesse in this art unattainable.

We had been given to understand that Penelope had never been broken-in, so when my ten-year-old granddaughter Lindsey came to stay at Easter I warned her about this. In a matter of hours I found Lindsey astride her in the field and Penelope completely unconcerned. The next thing was the devising of a makeshift bridle-halter, as we had no proper bridle small enough, and from here it was a small step to having Lindsey at heel on donkey-back when Copper and I went riding. One could hardly say that Lindsey was riding Penelope, as without a proper bit it was impossible for her to exert much control and Penelope would go where her whims took her, providing only that Copper remained in sight.

Natalka was not surprised when I told her about our exploits and the donkey not being broken. 'Surely donkeys never are?' she suggested, as if they were born with the sad burden of understanding their slavery to man. I did not know; these, the companion-helps of Copper, were the first donkeys to have come into my life.

During the winter I had kept in touch with the badgers whenever the nights were mild enough, watching by moonlight or torchlight – the badgers were accustomed to red-filtered torch beams. But at the best, winter watching is a cold and chancy business. It is not possible at this time of year to predict even within an hour or two the time of the badgers' emergence. Unlike the short nights of summer when hunger brings them out at the earliest moment, usually predictable within fifteen minutes or so, in winter they come out at their leisure, when they feel like it, or sometimes if the weather is very bad not at all (badgers do not hibernate in this country, but may spend as much as three nights underground in really adverse winter weather, living on layers of fat accumulated in the autumn).

It was not until early April that my watches became regular again; that is, on every reasonably fine night. For the first half of the month it was still torchlight watching. My hope of course was for the first sight of cubs. The earliest record I had for the Valley was March 30. On this year the date was April 8, a moonless night and dusk settling, when I experienced this never-failing enchantment. After all these years I never see the new cubs of the year for the first time without a feeling of thrill; and this was especially true now after the cubless years. On this night, after an earlier preliminary look-out, the boar and sow at the main sett came up into the open with one tiny cub. Under my fascinated gaze the sow began to groom the cub while the boar sat close by them. A woodcock was roding down the Valley with his strange chirr-squeak, and primroses shone in the grass, but I had little attention for them. This one small cub, because it was the first, made the highlight of a badger-watching year. The thought came to me that this might be the last time that I should see the first emergence of cubs in this valley.

Last year's cubs were still with the family, although fully grown now and approaching their first breeding season. I saw them often, but no more of any new cubs until April 14 when to my delight, at 8.15 B.S.T. in good daylight, a surge of badgers emerged complete with four cubs – the most I had ever seen together in the Valley. For a brief time they all played together, rolling and yelping and bouncing, until the cubs were ushered back underground and the grown-ups melted off into the woods.

These cubs took on a special value to me because of grievous events that spring to a badger family in a well-known Surrey garden open to the public. Often I had watched and photographed this family, entering the garden by special permission after the ordinary closing time. These badgers were old established and had been protected by earlier directors of the gardens, but in recent years I had felt that they were tolerated only. I did what I then thought was all that I could do, by letter and interview, to reinforce their protection, but still I remained uneasy. In this April the family was destroyed. I could not help feeling in some way guilty; as if, reluctant as we all are to be considered crankish, I had not pleaded for them sufficiently; had not perhaps kept a constant enough eye on them, in my preoccupation with our own cubs in the Valley.

The pity of it was that the badgers had done no real harm to this great garden, but probably much good in eating slugs and snails and rodents. Their sett was well hidden in trees and bushes in a wilder part of the garden, and although rhododendrons grew around and over it their growth and beauty was in no way affected.

Our family interested me particularly this spring because of their communal way of living. All nine, including last year's and this year's cubs, were behaving as a group. All played and foraged together, cubs and adults; several times when a blackbird chattered a warning I saw a yearling cub take a new one by the scruff and drag it down into safety. Blackbirds behave in what would be reckoned a neurotic manner in humans, one would suppose badgers to be familiar with their owl-panics and deer-panics and fox-panics; but when cubs are newly above ground badgers too are easily alarmed.

In what might be described as the north wing of this main sett complex a vixen was living. The four holes serving her quarters have no underground link with the adjacent main sett group. I had not seen fox-cubs yet, but now and again I saw the vixen going out at dusk. My old hope of watching fox and badger cubs playing together revived a little, but only a little, because of the obvious aversion that our badgers had always shown towards vixens in their area. Now, as in other springs, if the vixen was out and nearby the badgers did not emerge properly but would peer suspiciously from this hole or that, sniffing the wind and pulling back cubs who might poke out an adventurous muzzle. Because of this their emergence was often late; but with a moon rising and the watching at this time of year being so delightful anyhow, I was happy to sit waiting.

Since the beginning of some restrictions on the sale of pesticides the wild birds had become nearly as numerous as in our early years, filling the Valley with song and the small sound of wings. There was also for enjoyment the whole beauty of the spring woods, falling in torrents of bright beech-leaves to windflowers and wood sorrel beside the stream.

When the badgers did emerge there was much coming and going through the moonlit trees, bed-gathering and rollicking and foraging, and I longed to photograph it all but had devised no workable system that would not disturb their activities.

On May 6 there happened the strangest event I had yet seen in wild places. I was not alone as by some fortunate chance the Secretary of the Haslemere Natural History Society was already there on my ledges with a young man who was interested in badgers.

The evening began much as usual but earlier, the four cubs with two adults coming boldly from the main sett at 8.45. The cubs were growing rougher as they grew older and for about ten minutes there was much bouncing and yikking and grabbing each other's tails and whirling in circles. Then suddenly all was over and the family had submerged – as if there had been an air-raid warning – into underground safety. I looked into the flanking trees and saw the vixen's face at her squatter's earth under the beech tree, and then she too had gone underground.

For ten minutes the stage was deserted and we sat, a patient audience in the stalls, awaiting the return of the players. The first character in Act Two now appeared alone, the big boar, the father of the cubs; he was easily recognizable apart from his size by a white splash on his right flank. As if going to the Copse where the dung-pits were he walked up the path that passes the beech-tree holes, but to my surprise he went down into one of these entrances. In five minutes he was out again, carrying in his mouth a dead rabbit.

Trotting back along the path with the rabbit swinging he took it straight down into the sett. This was surprising. There is a wide-spread belief that badgers do not take food of any kind down into their setts. I remembered the moonlit night of the winter before last when I was certain that I had seen a rabbit taken down but decided that I must have been mistaken.

In ten minutes the boar emerged again. There had been no sign of the vixen, so that when he returned to her quarters and once more entered I watched with some suspense and excitement. For nearly twenty minutes our stage was empty. Then the boar rose out of the beech-tree entrance and I saw that he had the vixen limp and dangling in his jaws. The pity of it! Supposing there were cubs? But oh! for a tele-flash camera, the thoughts hit me as he carried her, his head held high to keep his burden off the ground; and she too was taken down into the sett.

My companions left soon after, since it seemed to them that the play was over. The young man as he was rising whispered to me, 'It's the first time I've seen wild badgers. It was very exciting! Is it always like this?'

I answered, 'No! What you have seen is so unusual, it may never have been recorded before.'

I stayed on: it was dark and the moon had risen before the family emerged again. Lethargic as banqueters who have fed too well, they sat about on the terraced ramp and contemplated the quiet Valley – quiet now as they had wished it to be. Had they eaten the vixen? I had little means of knowing; and now I was cold and stiff and it was time to go home: but I felt that I had seen natural history in the making.

Later I wrote to Dr Ernest Neal about it, and he replied that he had never heard of a similar incident. He was doubtful whether the boar had killed the vixen and suggested that she might have been a sick one or dead already, and the rabbit an offering from her mate. Events of the following spring were to put a different light on this, but until then it was to remain a mystery.

# CHAPTER SIXTEEN

FOR a few days after the taking of the vixen I kept a close watch on the fox-earth, anxious lest there should be orphan cubs which I could try to rear; but there were no signs of any, nor sounds within when I bent my ear to the holes.

On the evening after the incident a dog-fox came through the Valley. He paused for a minute at both the beech-tree hole and another serving the same quarters before trotting on downstream.

For a time the badgers seemed to take no further interest in this northern extension, but now came out much earlier, even in late sunlight, playing freely with the cubs all over the bank which had been the vixen's territory; but on the third night the sow badger went up to the beech hole and down into it. She remained inside for ten minutes or so before emerging by the hole from which both the rabbit and the vixen had been taken. There was nothing in her mouth. It would have seemed, then, that either there had been no fox-cubs or they had already been taken.

A friend of mine at the British Museum (Natural History), Geoffrey Kinns, listened with interest when he came down soon afterwards. He too had not heard of badgers killing foxes, but he did know of a vixen killing badger-cubs. This was something completely new to me and it was the first clue as to the badger's motive. Had this badger family lost cubs to a fox at some period, perhaps long past, and kept the knowledge of the danger? If so, I think it must be a localised danger, since reported incidents are so rare, whereas fairly often one hears of cubs of the two species playing together.

So beautiful was this May that I could hardly bear to miss any of it, and was rising early for watching and riding as well as roaming out late. During much of the day my time and care was for Bill, but early and late I was not needed. Before dawn I could go out to the

Valley, my feet making the same dark tracks through silver dew as the animals' did, to sit on my ledges and watch the mist melting upwards from the stream, and if I were lucky to see the badgers come home. Once in that May I watched a roe-buck wake. He was lying in the long grass where Valley field meets the woods, and I had not at first seen him because of his stillness and blending with the shadows. His rising gave him away and I watched him stretch, cat-like, his front legs extended, then lightly jump the dividing fence to come down to the stream. Because I was still he did not see me and thought he had all the Valley to himself. Pausing from time to time to nibble a twig or anemone leaf, he came leisurely down the steep bank and stood fetlock deep in the water to drink: I could see his muzzle wrinkling on the surface and the water circling his slender legs.

He came out on my side and waded in windflower and wood sorrel as if they were a different kind of water, rubbing his antlers on a little sapling, the velvet irritating him. When he went away, rubbing as he walked, he was exactly the colour of the woodland floor where the green did not reach.

Sometimes there was still time to ride before breakfast when I came home from the Valley. Mr Watkins grew used to seeing Copper trotting through the early morning trees to his garden gate. We would exchange greetings and news before I rode on through woods so fresh and silent it was difficult to imagine that anyone else existed in the world except the pony and myself.

Sean was home again now for the spring vacation. We talked about my photographic problems; how I felt that I should not any more work close enough to the badgers to disturb them, or to familiarize them with human presence, when perhaps in the near future we might no longer be able to protect them; and how Natalka and I had found working from the ledges impracticable.

Sean had a solution to my problems; almost certainly it would work and work well. All that it depended on was my willingness to spend what seemed a large sum of money – not for tele-flash, which if obtainable at all would be too expensive for my wildest dreams, but on a top-rating camera with a 400 mm lens. It was all very well messing about with an old twin-lens reflex when I was an amateur dabbler, he said, but it would not even take interchangeable lenses. Either I must remain a dabbler or equip myself properly as he had done for his botanical work. And as to the tele-flash, without which no lens would help much in those dim woodlands, he would make one for me; a custom-built job, and only for the cost of the components.

It might have seemed folly, my agreeing to this when our economic world was disintegrating around us, and even the very place and subjects of my work could still be taken from me, but I did agree, and fairly joyfully. With Sean I bought a Canon FT with through-the-lens meter and both the standard and a 400 mm lens. I had already a Metz 184 electronic flash-gun, which of course did not have the range needed for work from the ledges. I left Sean to buy all other components he needed, and these turned out to be three ordinary hand-lenses, such as are used for reading fine print, and some sheet perspex and adhesive.

Over the next week I watched the tele-flash take form on the kitchen table. When he had sawn the handles from the three lenses Sean next built a light carriage and ranged the lenses in series inside it. Behind them he made a perspex box in which my Metz flash fitted exactly, and the whole was mounted on a shoe to fit the camera. It sounds simple and in a way it was, as are so many of the best ideas, but it needed careful devising and accurate construction; and when it was completed it needed days more of careful testing in the woods where I was to use it. Between us we ran through several films while making precise notes of times and measurements and apertures and angles, and gradually our results began to excite us. The thing could be done!

Before the month was ended we had brought the system to what seemed to me near perfection, giving at least ten times the light intensity within the narrow angle of the telephoto lens. Sean maintained that it could be improved so that we could use fine-grained film or colour. Now using fast Tri-X film which we uprated to 1,600 ASA and developed accordingly, we were aiming the flash on to the precise focal point we selected and getting good results every time. We found that at first the adult badgers would dive at once when the flash was triggered (this may have been partly because of the audible shutter-click), but the cubs took no notice at all.

My badger watching evenings were revolutionized. Now I could capture on film almost anything that happened at and around the main sett when I was on the ledges. At first I felt drunk with the thrill and fascination of it, taking photographs all the time the badgers were in focus, sometimes as many as thirty in a night; but in time of course I settled to waiting for interesting events and groupings.

The adult badgers soon grew used to my activities and dived less quickly and often when the flash was triggered. Presently they, like the cubs, were taking no notice at all. Emboldened, I started getting them used to white torchlight, shielding it less each night until they were indifferent to a strong unfiltered beam. This made all the difference to the tricky job of focusing in twilight and dusk. Now I could spotlight my subjects and focus accurately at any time. If only, I thought, I'd had this system when the vixen was taken, I might have caught the wildlife photograph of the year.

Pleased with my pleasure in it, Sean still pointed out how far from ideal it was: we could not expect to get really good photographs, certainly not of exhibition quality, until we could use slower film and some kind of angled lighting to avoid flatness. To me it remained a joy, like suddenly being given a thoroughbred after years of riding a hired hack. Nightly now I would set forth to the Valley, burdened I admit with my equipment of camera, long lens, tele-flash and tripod; big torch, rubber cushion and field glasses; but even this was to be made easier for me, and in a completely unforeseen way.

This May one of the nicest and most extraordinary things happened to me, and it was particularly unlikely because it happened through the arrival of total strangers. I am shy about these and often experience an urge to bolt for the woods when I see the unfamiliar figures at the gate. This is silly because more often than not, once we are through the preliminaries, I am pleased to talk with someone who has made the effort to find our hidden farm just to tell me that a book of mine has given enjoyment.

This time I had no chance to escape because our visitors rang up and asked if they might call. They were from South Australia, a mother and grown-up daughter, on a pilgrimage to discover homes of their English ancestors, and also to find the settings and (where possible) authors of books they had enjoyed. Of course I said yes, by all means. And so, over coffee in the farm kitchen, we met Ruth Warland and her daughter Frances. It may sound like *The Man Who Came to Dinner*, but I cannot resist adding, at this moment more than a year later, that Frances is still with us, and I cannot imagine how ever I got on without her.

As I saw her on that first day – small, slight, very attractive with a halo of wavy honey hair, but quiet in manner – I put her age at about seventeen. I remember saying to Sean when suggesting that he left his studies to come and drink coffee with us, 'Now this is a really pretty one!'

The first of my surprises about Frances was to learn that she was a fully trained nurse, spending a summer touring England with her mother before going back to Australia to do her midwifery. This information called for the next astonishing fact; she was twenty-three. The two of them had hired a carawagon in which they were living and sleeping and travelling. The English traffic was going to take a lot of getting used to, Ruth Warland admitted, but the worst problem was parking, especially for a night. They were on a pull-in near Guildford at the moment, but it was rather noisy.

Little knowing what I was starting I said we should be happy if they would like to park for a few days in our quiet fields, from where they could explore a fairly wide area.

The carawagon went up into Yew Tree field and stayed there for a fortnight. At the end of this time, after many shared meals and walks and outings and much help from them both in the farmhouse, it seemed as if we had known them for years. Both of them were interested in the badgers – they had read my earlier badger book – and came with me to the Valley on many evenings, sharing the carrying of equipment. Their delight in seeing the cubs playing in sunlight under the beech trees was a pleasure in itself; as was all their delight in our green English spring with its seas of bluebells and wood anemones.

Often they would walk through the country by themselves when I was writing in the house, and it was on one of these walks that they heard shots close at hand in the Valley. They were near to the distant sett called the Outlier, where I knew there was a vixen with four cubs. As they stood looking through the trees a man with a gun and a yellow terrier went by carrying a dead fox.

When they told me, all of us were thinking of the cubs. Useless at this stage to speculate on what type of person would kill any animal while it was rearing young, leaving the little ones to a slow death by starvation, and all this on National Trust land. We decided to try to feed the cubs; and for the rest of the Warlands' fortnight we did this, taking out to the Valley each evening a trough of bread-and-milk with beaten egg and tinned cats' meat. It was always taken. Often we saw the fox-cubs, and they looked well.

While they were under our care all survived except one, and later I found this one dead in the woods further downstream. It had been dead too long for me to say how it had died, whether by shot or illness or perhaps the unfamiliar diet, which was the best I could provide and at least had probably saved three of the litter: often I would see these rollicking through the woods in the course of that beautiful summer.

As far as we were concerned the Warlands' van could have gone on staying all the summer in Yew Tree field, but Ruth said that if they didn't resume touring soon they would be flying back without finding any ancestral houses or seeing any more of Britain at all. We agreed that they should come back to the farm in August and stay with us – in the farmhouse this time – for their last two weeks. I wondered if, by that time, we should even own the farmhouse? But at least we should be here.

# CHAPTER SEVENTEEN

In some ways it was a sad summer, our hopes of selling the land without the farmhouse slowly diminishing. In other ways it was a summer of rare perfection and achievement. The achievement was Bill's. Characteristically, he had never accepted the idea of semi-invalidism: his daily cruises on the tractor were growing longer and he chafed at the neglect and desolation of the farm. With only Trellis and Copper and Penelope to graze them the fields were under a flood-tide of summer grass, and we knew that it should be cut for hay. I suggested hiring a contractor – what other solution was there, with Bill still far from his normal strength and constantly under hospital treatment? I should not have been much use myself, with a weak wrist and a deadline for finishing my book.

Bill swept aside my idea as economically unsound. He would hay the fields himself – gradually, he added, seeing my exasperation, a field at a time and working when he felt like it. It would do him good, he said; wasn't I the one who kept reminding him of his doctors' orders to exercise?

It was no good repeating that their idea of exercise was unlikely to be tractor-driving. Bill made the hay. His only concession was in hiring a baler and encouraging such family and friendly assistance as might be available. No further disaster struck him – I think if anything he gained in fitness – and wherever I walked and rode in that June and July the scent of his hay-making came with me and to meet me.

The perfection of those months was in the whole of that blue and gold summer; the foxgloves so many and steepling, the hedges creamed with elderflower blossom, the buttercups a cloth-of-gold in water-meadows where dragonflies flashed: but especially for me it was in those early rides, so quiet with the unshod hoofs pattering and birds and birdsong, and the dew silvering all the fields. I might see four roe deer in a deserted pasture, grazing peacefully like domestic cattle until looking up they saw the pony and rider and vanished like shadows; a fox crossing our path into the woods; cow-parsley foaming on to the track so that Copper's legs might have been drenched by its spray and not the dew.

The flies were bad, even at that early hour when the sun was level through the trees; I would lean and break off a bracken-stem and brush the pony's head with it. I leaned too to study tracks along the sandy paths – fox, badger, deer, even perhaps another pony – and guess how long since they were made. I might meet Mr Watkins coming up the narrow track in his van, on the way to Hindhead for his letters and groceries. Then, certainly, I should have to ride back to a woodland 'lay-by' and let him pass, for Copper would have gone mad if forced to meet such close traffic. From his refuge in the trees he would snort at the van with his eyes and nostrils popping, his ears almost meeting at their tips. When he was in this mood it felt like riding an Arab stallion, but when the van had rumbled away into the woods he would revert to peaceful plodding, the bracken-switch waving round his ears, until the turn homewards when excitement would break out again.

Now that the fields were silent with no cattle grazing, wild animals came into them more frequently. One June afternoon, with scents of hay and honeysuckle everywhere, I was with Haile in Lower Naps, picking elderflowers for wine, when we came suddenly on a roe doe curled asleep in the sun beneath the hedge. My shadow was nearly on her before she awoke and bounded through the long grass to the Valley with Haile gazing at her in astonishment, his puma-tail extended. I put my hands down in the oval nest she had left in the grass, and it was still warm. Often I had found these sleeping-nests of deer, before long grass was cut for hay, but never an occupied one before.

I think that the perfection of our countryside was heightened for me by the feeling of its almost inevitable loss; it was a true living of each day as if it would be the last. We were looking now at house-agents' advertisements; at houses too, and not liking what we saw.

In the middle of August the Warlands came back and joined us in the farmhouse for their last two weeks. It was during this time that Frances came to the conclusion that I needed a helper – so little writing done and the farm now at last coming on to the market – and somehow it was arranged, without our ever discussing it much, that she should stay behind when Ruth flew home to Australia. Even then I knew what luck had befallen me; but I was concerned for Frances, thinking how dull and lonely life would be for her, especially in the winter with only Bill and me for company; or how wretched it might be for her if we had to move to some unlikely district.

In the matter of my good luck I was right, but in fears about Frances being bored I could hardly have been more wrong. One thing she has in common with Natalka is a capacity to be interested in almost anything; at least in almost anything that I have been engaged in while she has been here. She is also content with a quiet life and solitude, in a way that still surprises me for such an intelligent and arrestingly pretty girl. By early September she was as much a member of our family as any of us. She had somehow acquired, and without any of us intending it, the nickname of Goldie. It came about after I had said, watching a television programme, 'I like our Goldie best.' We all tried to avert this new baptism when we saw it imminent, but already it was too late. We made efforts to revert to her real name, but she was Goldie.

Now the whole farm with its land and its old house and buildings – our home for twenty-two years – was on offer to anyone who would buy it. To me this month was terrible and funny and sad and joyful in its different aspects. It would have been exhausting too except for Sean and Goldie, who buffered me from so much of the publicity and many of the inquirers resulting from advertisements in country magazines and daily papers. All day, it seemed, we were to have strangers and the phone would be ringing. All kinds of people were to make the journey to our lonely place; the day-dreamers, the speculators, the cranks, the serious buyers and the merely curious; reporters and fans and sympathisers and proposition makers. Whenever they could Sean and Goldie sorted and sifted them all, so that Bill and I would not be harrowed and bothered. And in the evenings there was still the Valley and the badgers, and the fascination of my focused flash camera system, to keep all of us sane and in some kind of touch with the 'serene silence that lies at the heart of things'. In the Valley in those September evenings it was easy to keep peace with one's soul.

Although we had not meant to break through the badgers'

survival barriers of wildness and suspicion, since our protection seemed almost certain to be withdrawn from them, it seemed as if in these last days of summer they had broken through them for themselves. Still keeping to our intention not to watch very near them we went always to the ledges across the stream, or to the woods above the setts, keeping our distance. But the badgers did not keep their distance; sometimes it seemed as if they had come out of their way to find us.

Once when Goldie and I were on the ledges with equipment all around us and white torch blazing, the cubs – half-grown now – came down to the stream, splashing through it with the gusto that, of all wild animals, only badgers seem to have in such abundance. Straight up our side of the Valley they came, bounding up the steps that I had made, to pass by us almost in touching distance, with only a brief pause to glance at our glare of light and shining tripod and our faces watching them. Even our scent drifting closely did not trouble them and they went carefree up into the woods behind us where we could hear them foraging in the leaf-soil.

This was about the time when Legs Selassie started his long love affair with the Wild Valley. He had begun to follow us down there on daytime walks in August, clearly fascinated by the place and always reluctant to leave it and come home. Although continually urging us to set out and go with him there – running up the track towards the fields whenever we went out of the door, and looking back over his shoulder with a cry that sounded like, 'Now! Now!' – he became less willing to return with us. Sliding off like a ghost into the trees he would vanish out of sight and hearing. For the rest of the day he would stay down there, but when in the dusk we returned from our evening watches he would bound out from the trees and join us.

Once when he was not at the Valley gate to greet us I stood and called him, 'Haile! Haile!' There was a padding in the dark woods and to our astonishment out trotted the three badger cubs. Gazing at us for a minute in apparent interest – as we were at them – they shook their heads and trotted on past us to vanish in rustles of leaves and bracken on their way to the south woods. A moment later Haile answered my call and came out of the darkness.

There was the evening, too, when Goldie watched alone in the woods above the setts while I was on the ledges. My friend Aileen

Haile began hunting on a considerable scale

Sitting soberly on the ramp

Arwen took bread-and-milk from offered dishes

The cubs would climb well clear of the ground

Grisewood was with me and we had been watching the badgers hunting out raisins and peanuts that we had hidden around for their – and our – enjoyment. When the last raisin had been discovered and disputed and champed, the badgers filed up into Valley field out of our sight and we along the stream homewards.

From the stream-crossing there is a grassy glade leading steeply through the woods to the gate into the fields. These were the woods where Goldie was watching, and we paused below the gate to see if she were coming: she would have noticed the switching off of our torch across the Valley. As we looked through the shadowed trees she came into our sight walking quietly. Behind her, as close as though trotting at heel, were the badger cubs. And not only the cubs, I now saw, but the sow as well. It was a kind of Elysian Pied Piper scene, the golden girl walking through the woods with wild animals freely following: it was, and remains, one of the truly astonishing things that I have seen in years of watching wild animals. We had done nothing to entice or tame them: any offerings we had brought had been handled only with gloves and hidden earlier in the day; but we were often in the Valley and our scent was probably known to them.

When Goldie came near, the sow badger saw us and halted. Perhaps one human was all right but three were too many: or perhaps Aileen's scent was less well known to her. She turned, not hurrying, back into the woods again, and the cubs went with her: but one looked back over his shoulder and lingered for a moment. Then all were gone.

I said that this month seemed terrible and funny and joyful and sad. The offering of our farm on the market was not the most terrible thing. There had been a pause in the succession of lively and exotic cards from Natalka on her travels with Nicholas in Turkey, and then came a last card, posted in London – *There has been a fearsome accident, with fearsome consequences . . .*

In a few days there was more news. Their expedition van had crashed in Yugoslavia. Only she and Nicholas were in it. She had escaped with lesser injuries but Nicholas had broken his back. He was in Stoke Mandeville Hospital, where he would be for several months, and he would never walk again.

To us this seemed utter disaster. We did not know the tenacity and courage of Nic. It seemed like the end of a brilliant career, cut off in the young years. Perhaps Natalka guessed, but we didn't, that a broken back would not be enough to stop Nicholas.

I wrote to her at once; her old room was waiting for her; it was hers for as long as she liked, and we would love to have her. My guess that she too needed care and that her empty house was no place for her, proved true, although she would not be able to come to us until the middle of October.

# CHAPTER EIGHTEEN

THE funny aspects of that September were mixed up with its dark ones, in that they were gleams in the awfulness of showing prospective buyers over one's private and personal place. 'Yes, I do write in this room . . . My husband has a ground-floor bedroom since his accident . . . The bathroom door *is* rather low . . . No, I don't know why there is a window in the loo-door, but it's easy to curtain it . . . The floor is rather humped, but we like it . . . '

There were many unlikely people, even among those whom I escorted; there were others whom I never saw – people who did not seem to fit the farm, nor the farm to fit their lives and careers. They were, mostly, escapers from noise and crowding: if a peaceful place could be found (but not too far from London) they would make their careers fit into it. Some did not want the land, as land, but only as a buffer against the world. The idea that it might need to be cared for, if it were not to tumble down to weeds and scrub, was a new one to the urban mind which thought of grass as a permanent feature, self-maintaining.

I remember one such viewer noticing Bill's bee-hives near the yew tree and saying with the air of one solving an obscure problem, 'Oh, you have bees! If we kept bees we shouldn't have to do anything about the fields, should we?'

We had a rose-grower and a trout-farmer; a lady racehorse trainer who mystified me by saying she would have to 'stone' the Wagon Track (only afterwards did my battered mind realize that she meant pick the stones off it); there was a breeder of skewbald donkeys, and a handsome man whose eyes blinked independently, and a lady who left her white peke in the Rolls-Royce and tore up her chauffeur when it barked. So many people; so many white Rover 2000s, for some odd reason; so many automatic responses from ourselves – 'Yes, it is rather low, isn't it?' . . .

Among the most memorable of our viewers were two Beatles. George Harrison was the first, arriving unexpectedly in a white Mercedes with his young wife Pattie Boyd. It was naturally impossible not to recognize them, and we presently said so as they shared our tea in the farm kitchen, but they seemed to us unaffected and likeable people. Sean walked with them round the fields after they had seen the house, and they came back saying that although the house was too small for their own needs it was probably exactly what a friend of theirs was looking for.

When Sean told us the next day that Paul McCartney was on the phone we looked at him disbelievingly, but it was so; and presently his Aston Martin was sliding through our gate. He had brought Linda, his American wife, and their tiny baby Beatle who stayed asleep in the car while they sat together on the sofa holding hands and gazing at the logs burning in the open fire-place, with Pardos on Paul's knee, as they told us what they were looking for. More than anything it was peace and simplicity, the balancing needs in a life such as theirs. They wanted a quiet and solitary place, small and unsophisticated, where their children could live 'like ordinary country kids' and where Linda could ride unnoticed. They had a place like that in Scotland, but it was too far for sudden brief escapes.

I showed them over the house ('Is this the only bathroom?' Paul asked, and I wondered about our different definitions of the term 'sophisticated'); they walked with Sean round the fields and Valley, and came back I think a little in love with it all, for all its shortage of bathrooms. They did not want to farm the land, Paul said; they wanted to put a covenant on it and make it into a Nature Reserve for ever. I was very interested in this as conservation is almost a religion to me. In Scotland, Paul said, they had taken 1,000 acres of shooting – just to stop shooting.

We talked about the wildlife in this Valley and in the miles of common and woodland around it, and we looked at some of my photographs. Linda told me that in Arizona she had sometimes ridden all day and not seen a house or a road. She talked to me about bobcats and pumas, in a soft slow voice that seemed almost shy, and to Sean about cameras – she was in England as a professional photographer when she met Paul.

They came back a few days later by train – second class – and country bus, walking the last mile and a half from the bus stop. It was a day of autumn mist and they came through it strolling up the drive hand in hand. I said, 'Is it because you think people won't recognize you, or you know they will but they'll think it can't be you?'

'They always think it can't be,' Paul said, 'and we like that. We like trains and buses and walking, too.'

We sat talking for a while and they decided they would like to go on walking, in the fields and woods. 'If you're sure you won't get tired?' Paul asked Linda, and said to me, 'It's only three weeks since the baby was born.'

I offered the services of Copper and Linda was delighted. We went up to my room and rummaged for jeans for her, and while she changed I saddled Copper and brought him round. I went with them through the first field to make sure that they knew the direction, and at the gate into Upper Naps I watched them disappearing happily into the mist towards the Wagon Track with Paul walking beside the pony.

We were rather a crowd at tea as apart from ourselves there was our usual complement of resident friends, so it was a good thing that Trellis had calved and was supplying milk and cream and butter ('Did Trellis make this?'); and everyone was talking at once as usually happens here, and Paul wanted to tell us a story about his Dad playing the trumpet but could not make himself heard – 'Listen, just *listen!*' he said, and it was just the same as if he had been one of our lot.

We talked about music and songs and singing, and I said how I liked *Eleanor Rigby*, and Paul sang me a fragment of it over the egg-cups and explained how he had written it; and Linda sat back with her hand across Paul's knee and said, 'Do you know, this is the first place since I left America where I've felt really relaxed.'

They would have walked back as they came the mile and a half to the bus, but Sean offered to drive them, and on the way down the lane Paul tossed at Sean an offer for the farm, and it eclipsed anyone else's by a fairly impregnable margin.

So it might have been, except for the intervention of a new and unique proposition from someone I will call Mr Brown. This was to rebuild the old fallen wing of the farmhouse and rent it complete with its own garden to Bill and me and allow me the continued use of the Valley. Although the price we should receive for the farm was considerably lower than Paul McCartney's figure, this offer was overwhelmingly tempting – at least to me, with my work and interests and pleasure so much involved in the Wild Valley and the countryside around it. We had for weeks been investigating properties for sale, as far away as Dorset, and had found nothing that we could both afford and care about.

Bill and I therefore accepted Mr Brown's offer with much pleasure and relief that we should not need to be uprooted, and interest too in the whole idea of seeing the rebuilding of the old wing. It was not until much later that a new condition was put before us: it was that the lease of the wing should be for five years only, then to be renewable annually by agreement of both parties. This was of course completely unacceptable to us as it might have meant that in five years we should again be hunting for a home.

Mr Brown pointed out that an 'open-ended' lease would be equally unacceptable to him since Bill and I might grow old and he unable to remove us.

We were still in a state of deadlock when a completely unforeseen and astonishing thing happened. The Planning Committee decided to reconsider our year-old application to build a house in the Little Orchard. We had made no appeal against their earlier refusal, nor any fresh application. I had, in fact, written to them approving of their decision against us, since for all our personal hardship I was glad to think that the countryside was being so staunchly protected against more building.

The mystery as to what had influenced the Committee to re-open our case remained unanswered for some time as we awaited the date of their next meeting in early December, but meanwhile we ended our negotiations with Mr Brown. The whole aspect of the farm sale would be changed if permission to build were granted, since permission this time would have to be for a house for our retirement; it was too late now to think of starting up the farm again.

When Natalka came to us in October I was shocked to see how ill she looked. Goldie and I kept her in bed as much as we could, with pillows and books and hot-water bottles; it seemed to us that what she needed was rest and as much freedom from responsibility as possible, and these were fairly easy for us to provide. Natalka was a perfect guest and patient, fitting as easily into our household as she had always done when she was strong and well. I was worried about her post-concussion headaches, but gradually these improved and she began to resume her old active part in the farmhouse life. The windfall apples, which usually I made into wine but now had no heart to deal with, started her off. She swept aside my excuses and went out to gather them from the lawn, and under my instructions began a great wine and chutney making that would rejoice us all in the months of stress ahead of us.

In the evenings there were log fires and music, and nightly telephone contact with Nicholas at Stoke, and a new activity for us of making rugs. The first one took the form of a simple hooked rug based on an earlier kneeler design of leaping dolphins. Natalka and I made this together fairly indiscriminately, one of us carrying on where the other left off, so that now I do not know which part of it is hers and which mine. We played all our records and tapes, or watched the flames and listened to the silence, and when Natalka began to gain strength we beguiled her into telling us more of her war and expedition adventures, in her incomparable way. 'Home was a fortress; we had 200 horses to defend, as well as all the men and their families,' she might begin, and we were away into experiences so electrifying that time went unnoticed, and I regretted again the reminiscences that probably never would be written.

At their first meeting in December the County Planning Committee approved our application and gave us provisional planning permission. This was by no means absolute since it was the first of many hurdles in the granting of final detailed planning permission, but it was the main hurdle without which the others were not even approachable. Now we heard how it was that we had been granted a fresh consideration. My sister – always known to the family as Dofey – had in the goodness of her heart written to them saying how she thought our case so exceptional that if they understood they must reconsider it. We had not the faintest idea of this, nor even that she had thought of it, but her letter must have been a masterpiece of advocacy for it swung the balance in our favour. Except for it the Committee probably would never have thought of us again and we most likely would soon have been far away from Punch Bowl Farm.

Now with this first critical meeting behind us it was impossible not to meet the New Year with cheerfulness and optimism. There were to be four meetings (since both the County and Rural District Councils were involved) at monthly intervals before we could possibly begin building, and then only if all the meetings approved. We, and Dofey, were sure that they would approve; but meanwhile the sale of the farm was suspended. When finally it was offered again the conditions might be very different, for if we were to retain a half acre for building we could also retain the Wild Valley, and this was a giddy thought after the months of conditioning myself to let it go.

# CHAPTER NINETEEN

EXCEPT for a brief visit to Cambridge to receive her M.A. Natalka was with us until Nicholas came home in February. A typically laconic postcard arrived from Cambridge; *Been made an M.A. O.K.*, to be followed by Natalka herself, looking so much better now than she had done in October that we were reassured about letting her go home. Our confidence was reinforced by Nicholas himself, as independent and active a person in a wheelchair as I suppose I shall see in all my life, resuming his work as an oceanographer, delivering lectures and attending banquets as he had always done and driving himself in an enormous manually operated Chrysler. All of us had to learn right away that help was not acceptable or needed unless called for, and this was seldom. Presently I was to see him negotiating in his wheelchair a flight of twelve steps, unaided, and diving again with an aqualung: but meanwhile the winter dragged on with its weary waiting. It would have seemed longer except for Goldie.

I think now of how she shared all our strains and pressures as she shared our interests, so that I cannot imagine how we ever got on without her. It was Goldie who came out with us in the middle of the dreadful night when Trellis suddenly fell ill, helping Bill and me to dose her and keep her head up, and when Trellis died as the vet's headlights came through the gate it was Goldie who consoled us.

She is good at joining in and doing things with one, or at taking up and completing things that one has abandoned. She caught photography at once from Sean and me, and now she had her own Canon camera with standard, wide-angle and zoom lenses, and had learned to develop my uprated films for me. She took over from me the completion of the Cathedral kneeler of Cosford Mill – a design of swans and mill-wheels and wheat for our friends the Loarridges – and she was teaching herself cooking with such success that before the winter was out she was making the most superb apple pies.

In the mornings as I lay luxuriously in bed before breakfast listening to music, Goldie would bring the house to life: I would hear her feeding the hens, and her own wild birds which came to the windows, and getting breakfast ready for us in the kitchen. January was glorious and we walked through fields and woods in warm sunshine – my riding was over; we had parted with Copper and Penelope when the farm was up for sale. Goldie teased us about the English winter – 'Deep and crisp and even?' – and I said, 'You wait! We have this thing called February.' But most of February was lovely, too; the winter did not really strike until we were almost in March. We had real snow then and she loved it.

By the middle of February we knew that the planning committees were in our favour and that it was likely only to be a matter of time before our final permission came through. We placed the farm back on the market, but retaining this time the half acre for building as well as the Wild Valley. At this point Mr Brown came back on the scene. Our agents advised us to pick up negotiations with him rather than launch on a fresh campaign of advertising with its concomitant of general publicity and applicants to view. This we did, but soon I learned to my sorrow that any deal with him entailed the loss of the Valley; he would proceed only on that condition.

It was only to me that the Valley and its wildlife mattered so much; they were not important to Bill: and Mr Brown was prepared, as before, to allow me a lifetime's access and to avoid disturbance of the wildlife there. After a day or two's struggle with myself I came to the conclusion that it would be wrong for me to be obstructive on this point, causing delay and expense and some distress to all of us, and I agreed to let the Valley go; but I knew that no one else could understand how hard that decision was.

Goldie and I meanwhile had a new interest. After the preliminary stage of the dolphin-pattern hooked rug we became interested in finer rugs and were reading everything we could find on the history and making of oriental carpets. We studied the genuine article wherever we found it, in shops and museums and friends' houses, and we traced and visited an expert maker who kindly offered to instruct us. With graph paper and pencil we devised designs based on but different from the illustrations in our books and finally, acquiring canvas, fine wools, dyes and needles, we were launched.

This was bold of us, bearing in mind our ages, for we had read that the best oriental carpet makers have always been girls under seven; after this age their fingers coarsen and their attention wanders as they become preoccupied with thoughts of love! Whenever our work seemed further than usual from perfection Goldie and I would say to each other, 'I must be in a very over-sevenish mood this evening,' or, 'Six stitches wrong – well, what can we expect, at our ages?'

As is no doubt usual in writers I began thinking in terms of a new book; how delightful it would be to travel with a notebook and camera through carpet-making countries while this industry is still carried on by hand, and devise a book about it.

The spring found us only an inch or two advanced with our own industry, so fine and slow is the work, but the fascination was such that evening carpet making to music and a wood fire gave place only to watching in the Valley as the weather allowed it; after the genial winter the spring was exceptionally delayed and cold with nine weeks of sub-normal temperatures.

Our negotiations with Mr Brown were also disappointingly delayed. In view of the earlier searches and discussions we had hoped for an exchange of contracts in March or early April, but this was not to be. We little guessed what was ahead of us in this line.

Goldie, whose talents I think were wasted on me and should have found a wider field, continued to help and amuse and console us. Her real intention in staying with us was to free me for writing, so that for the first time in over twenty years I should be able to write in the mornings when I am fresh and alert, and not late in the evenings when energy and inventiveness flag. For a long time I could not avail myself of this unique opportunity; the pressures were such that I seemed unable to write anything at all.

At about this time one of my life's pleasantest surprises happened to me. During the winter I had developed an affection for a pair of large plaster Egyptian cats which had appeared on the gateposts of a Surrey antique shop. They were beautiful and expensive. Based on a statue in the British Museum they sat upright and arrogant, their high ears pointed, their elegant shoulders circled with a 'gold' chain (as Haile's was with his dark necklet) and I lusted after them, greeting them from the car when we passed their gate and naming them Isis and Osiris. (I remember the pleasure and amusement one day of seeing a bottle of milk left at the feet of Osiris by the morning milkman.)

Then came an April morning when I looked out of my window early and looked again. I called to Lindsey, on a holiday visit and sharing my room: she scrambled out of her camp-bed and we gazed together. There were my Egyptian cats, sitting one each side of our garden gate: cloaked in brown paper and string they surveyed the morning, guarding the old house. Completely mystified and a little exalted I rushed down to uncloak them, to gaze and to collect the family and speculate.

Eventually on a process of elimination I telephoned Natalka: 'A mystery has happened at the farmhouse!'

'Oh, what mystery?' Surely she was hedging? I remembered the Easter before last, when she had crept in during the small hours and left a clutch of coloured eggs in a hen-house nest box and feigned astonishment when asked about it.

It was Natalka of course. She and Nicholas had thought of it as a thank offering for our care of Natalka while he had been in Stoke – as if we needed any for such a guest. Nicholas later told me about it: with a friend they had brought the cats late in the evening. 'It was great fun, rather like a military operation, or being at school again.' They had not dared to use the car lights and there was no moon. The car had to be kept very quiet, the engine ticking over, and the doors opened some hundred yards distant. They saw to their dismay that we were still up, with lights and music in the sitting room. The gate squeaked as it was opened; the cats were heavy, even for Natalka and a strong accomplice. Nicholas would not let the car doors be shut and they drove away feeling like agents on a desperate adventure.

Incredibly, with Shelley's two dogs in the sitting-room, neither they nor we ever heard a thing. Such are the powers of music.

Bill said in the morning, 'We'll have to put in a bigger cat-door, now.'

Rover peered at the guardians with extended muzzle, ready for flight. We admired the ear-rings that Nic and Natalka had fitted: and then I found a postcard showing the original cat which Goldie had once brought me from a visit to the British Museum; I felt that I could spare it now and I sent it to Nic and Natalka: 'Isis and Osiris send you greetings. They would tell you that they have been received with ceremony, and have accepted their appointment as Guardians of the House.'

In the early spring our Valley watches were usually shared by Haile and Rover. Often Haile was already down there, having defected from an afternoon walk with us. We were still watching from the ledges, my old fear of taming the badgers too much and making them vulnerable having returned with the renewed prospect of losing the Valley. Half afraid for Haile after what had happened to the vixens I devised a way of calling him up to us without familiarizing the badgers with my voice – I remembered how the cubs had come out from the woods when I had called Haile in the autumn. I found that all the cats quickly responded to a loud mouse squeak, although the badgers took little notice of it, and so the squeaking-up of any woodland cats became the routine preliminary to most of our watches.

Haile's enchantment with the Wild Valley came over him again that spring, so that he was always running up the stone steps to the track with his cry of, 'Now! Now!' whenever we went out of the house. Eventually we really would be setting out for the Valley and not to the hens or the clothes line, and he would run ahead joyfully but with back-slung ears, looking round to be sure that we were coming. On our return he would accompany us to the gate out of the woods and then melt back silently into the trees and the bracken, to stay there however much we called him, until the evening's badger watch. Although he liked our company on the outward journey he is a very independent cat, not inclined to such softnesses as knee-sitting and allowing himself to be carried.

Haile now began hunting on a considerable scale, his catches ranging from mice to rabbits, but his usual bag was short-tailed voles. He would kill these quite expertly, to our relief, and then throw them about in an ecstasy of play. They were of course liable to land anywhere, and I remember one that landed *inside* the electric toaster on a table. Luckily we had seen it landing. Squeaking him up in the Valley he was liable to appear through the trees with the hindquarters of a rabbit or a squirrel in his jaws.

At about this time a slowly growing feud between Pardos and Haile exploded into recurring fights of some ferocity. Pardos was nearly always the aggressor, his schizophrenic tendencies becoming so marked that he seemed seldom to know whether he was feeling more sentimental than hostile or vice versa. Haile's solution was in more frequent escapes to the Valley, where he seemed truly to belong, blending like a wild animal into the surroundings.

We had to be very careful never to have Pardos and Haile in the Valley together, so as not to destroy his sense of refuge there. When Rover fell in behind us on our evening expeditions we knew that Haile would be at his best. Already in the Valley he would come bursting out of the trees in a rapturous state to greet us, and rush madly about pouncing on dead leaves or on Rover indiscriminately, slithering and even rolling down the Valley side in an uproar of avalanches and calling to us all the time. Sedate and kindly tolerant in the heaven of his domestication Rover would sit like a rock assaulted by waves, or wander off silently into the dusk on missions of his own; but until Haile settled down or accompanied him there would be little hope of seeing any wildlife. We would sit listening to the evening chorus of songbirds and gazing at the young leaves and a surf of anemones as one does at things precariously owned and soon to be lost for ever.

Rover displayed a total indifference to the badgers, as he did to the tribe of five fox-cubs which presently appeared, as last year, at the beech-tree hole. He would peacefully wash himself, looking the other way as the fox-cubs loudly rioted or the belated badgers sat scratching on their ramp; the badgers, again as last year, deferring their emergence until the fox-cubs had gone away or back underground. Haile once rushed the emerging boar who retired at once, not sure of the identity of his noisy assailant. I had to get Goldie to take Legs Selassie home in the interests of his own safety.

On May 3 we saw the first badger-cub. He was a big sturdy one for so early in the year and he came out close behind his mother at five past nine, after the fox-cubs had gone to earth again. I took several photographs with the tele-flash as he rooted with the sow for peanuts we had scattered there, and neither he nor his mother took much notice. The cub boisterously blundered about, twice falling into a 'cave' that may once have been a sett entrance, and I hoped that he was not the only one in this year's family.

On the next evening, after a perfect afternoon in which with Rover we had watched the fox-cubs and a roe doe in full sunshine, a terrible thing happened.

I was there alone and early with the camera hoping to get shots of the fox-cubs. Although their beech hole was out of reasonable range even for the 400 mm lens there was a chance that in their play the cubs would come closer. Three were already out, but instead of playing wildly as usual they were sitting soberly on the ramp outside the earth. I should have realized that something was wrong, but I did not. I supposed that they were waiting for the other two cubs to join them. Very still and solemn they sat there, as if listening to something happening in the earth. Experimentally I took two photographs, knowing that the cubs could only be very small on the negative, and waited, gazing as if in a dream at the spring-green trees. As so often, dreaminess was my downfall, leading to total unpreparedness as the cubs rose turning to stare at the hole, out of which burst like a depth charge the boar badger with the vixen struggling in his jaws.

I should have known, I should have expected it: it was May 6, two days later than the date last year when I had seen a vixen taken from this same earth; but unprepared I was unable – try as I would, and how I tried! – to realign and refocus the camera before the boar had galloped down the short path to the main sett and dived, with the vixen thrashing, down into the north entrance. At the distance where I was it would have been impossible to try to save the vixen, even if she had not been mortally injured.

The fox-cubs scattered wildly into the woods. I was never to see these five again at the beech earth, and never more than three together in other parts of the wood. Haile had been with me but had gone off into the trees and did not see this drama; so I sat alone on the ledges with my useless camera – which had I only been alert could have caught for me a picture of great interest and rarity – and seethed with pity and frustration and regret and excitement and wonder.

Now twice I had seen a vixen taken from the beech hole and down into the main sett. This time I had no witness, but I had learned more. This vixen was not a sick one but large and strong, and she had been alive and fighting. However peaceably some badgers and foxes may live close together, the badgers of our Valley were not prepared to tolerate foxes close at hand and would take extreme measures to get rid of them.

Another spring, I decided, if a vixen took over the beech hole I would evict her to save the lives of herself and her cubs. Meanwhile all that could be done was to try to save these cubs, as we had done with the Outlier litter. I squeaked up Haile, fearful now for his own life, and went home to tell the story of this new woodland tragedy to Goldie.

Her parents clearly accepting her

A regular meals-in-trough service

Arwen came closest of all

Arwen ate from our bare hands

# CHAPTER TWENTY

IN the middle of May to our joy the expected final planning permission came through and work began on the foundations for a one-storied house in the Little Orchard; but although nearly three months had now passed since the renewal of negotiations with Mr Brown, matters were proceeding slowly.

We tried to set anxieties aside in the belated though quite perfect spring. Often I would be up very early – perhaps 3.30 a.m. – to see badgers and deer in the unwary pre-dawn hour, to photograph the sun lancing through dewy dandelions and grasses; and sometimes to my pleasure to see the three fox-cubs leaping through the young bracken. It was good to know that they were still alive, although never taking the food we left for them and not going near the beech-tree earth from where their mother had been taken, and where now cobwebs hung across the entrance.

Once on one of these early mornings a cuckoo flew across the Valley, calling his two well-known notes *and also* the bubbling call associated with the female. So now I knew from my own observation that the same bird can make both the cuckoo calls.

Now that the fox family had gone the badgers became much more relaxed and confident, as they had done last year, emerging earlier and playing under the beech trees. For a few days Goldie and I saw only the one big cub, whom we came to know as Bully Boy, but soon three smaller ones emerged all together – a different family? – and lastly, some days later, a fifth, very small.

All the cubs tended to play and forage together with all the adults, as in previous years, but usually they emerged in the order I had first seen them; Bully Boy first, then the three middle ones and then the very small cub, which in spite of a feminine head we thought might be a male because of the sparse tail usual to boars. Even allowing for the delays and uncertainties with Mr Brown the following weeks were pure happiness from the point of view of two country people like Goldie and me. Often as we walked down Lower Naps towards the Valley one of us would suddenly exclaim what became nearly our cliché, 'Oh, what a lovely life we lead!' And I would think how good it was that we knew this now, while we were living it, instead of thinking from the remote standpoint of future years, 'We *did* have a good life, didn't we?'

The badger family responded readily to the peanuts and raisins we raked into the leaves for them, and the honey-scrapings which we spread on roots and low branches. Every evening, from our theatre stalls across the stream, we were treated to such a performance of play and squabbling and grooming and affection and general riotousness as might last the average badger watcher a whole season. No notice whatever was taken of us (the Lightning Throwers, Goldie said we were) as torch and flash were confidently used. Often I could take a dozen or more photographs in an evening and once, I see in my notes, on a night of bed-gathering and digging and much wild cub play, I took thirty-six, a whole film, returning with an empty camera at 9.30 when the badgers were still around the sett.

The cubs would swing on the low branches after our honey, often falling off with a plop into the leafmould: one oak tree, known to us as the Honey Tree, they would climb well clear of the ground, straight up the trunk, for honey smeared there. In a trance of fascination with their wild world we would watch them, among trees full of songbirds and a woodpecker drumming and the roe buck barking down the Valley.

Often Rover would be sitting peacefully beside us or on Goldie's knee, and Haile would be setting off his ecstatic avalanches among the trees.

On the morning of June 16 we had a phone call from a neighbouring farmer to say that a badger-cub had been found unconscious but still alive in one of his fields. Goldie and I went at once to see what could be done. The cub – a very small sow – was lying where he had put her by his gate. She looked far gone, with eyes glazed and half open, her breathing too shallow to be noticed. I picked her up and put her into my clothes, and she was so cold, it seemed that there was no warmth in her.

We thought as we walked home that she might be the very small cub of our Valley clan, and that being so much smaller than the others she had somehow been left behind on a night's foraging and succumbed to the coldness – the night temperature had been unseasonably low. Our neighbour thought that she belonged to different badgers living in a sett in one of his hedges; but we knew from our watches that this sett was an outlying one occasionally used by our badgers, and that at this time no other family lived there, nor anywhere else on these two farms.

We took the cub up to my bedroom and made a hay-box nest for her, with a hot-water bottle and warm towels constantly renewed. In the early afternoon I had to go with Bill to hospital. The cub was still unconscious and Goldie took over the care of her; once again there was an Intensive Care Ward in the farmhouse. Some three hours later as I returned I looked up and saw Goldie at my window. The cub would be dead, and she was going to break it to me gently – that was why she was smiling. Somehow the reviving of the cub had become very important; I even had in a corner of my mind a name for her – Arwen, Evenstar, from *The Lord of the Rings*.

"She's all right!' Goldie called down to me in the garden. 'She's been out of her box and all round the room, and she took honey and raisins from my fingers!'

Arwen was back in her hay-nest when I came into the room, but her eye as she looked at me was bright and black. I could see her strong breathing with no difficulty at all. Goldie and I hugged each other in a triumph of delight and achievement and she told me how, slowly, life and warmth had come back into the small body, until finally the cub had heaved herself out of her hay-box. I said how I had thought of her as Arwen, because her time – if she lived, as we were sure she would – would always be the time of the evening star; and Goldie was pleased: it was she who had introduced Sean and me to J. R. R. Tolkien's masterpiece which now we had read twice through – all three volumes – without break.

'I'm sure she's one of ours,' Goldie said; 'knowing about honey and raisins!'

Very slow and quiet movements were necessary from us; she froze in horror at a sudden gesture, gazing at us with her bright button eyes. She had beautiful white-tipped ears and a delicate feminine muzzle dished upwards, but her coat was thinner than I should have expected – inadequate for lying out on cold nights – and her tail was so sparse and scrawny and carried sideways that it was hard to believe she was a female. I thought about the tail of the small fifth cub in the Valley, and more and more felt that this was she. Too small to keep up on family Walk About she had got left behind and deeply chilled, to a state of hypothermia.

After taking cats' meat and bread-and-milk from offered dishes – she had to wrinkle her muzzle to get these foods, with her badgers' underset jaw – she settled back into her nest, refusing water, and went to sleep again covered with hay and her warm towel. Goldie and I went out to see if we could establish for certain where she belonged.

On that first evening we kept watch near the sett where she had been found, but no badgers appeared there, and a later examination showed no recent tracks around the sett. It was a period of long drought and the fields were very dry: we thought that the badgers had probably gone there visiting perimeter setts as is usual when cubs begin to be active, but had found poor foraging in the hard ground and gone back to the stream. The next night we would watch in the Valley.

Arwen took more meat and warm milk at about half-past ten, and returned to her box. I left a peat-box near by and some food and milk, and went to bed across the room from her. She got up twice in the night and I could hear her eating and drinking. I also heard her messing, I was not sure where, but my torch showed her in the peat-box. She took no notice of the torch – another indication that she was one of the Valley badgers – but climbed back into her box and humped the hay up on top of her. It was a strange and memorable experience, badger-watching by torchlight from the comfort of one's bed.

At dawn she got up in earnest. After eating and drinking she began great efforts to go home before it was really daylight, trundling round and round the room, trotting at times, and trying every way to get out. She got stuck behind a chest of drawers and cried, and I went across and pulled the chest from its corner. She thought her peat-box might be a way out and began digging in it, throwing the peat out; I could hear her strong claws on the bottom of the box. She went several times behind the bookcase – a tight fit – and pushed out heavy books on to the floor: I pulled the bookcase out for her. I moved out of her way the trolley with my tape recorder on it, and finally I stood naked as I was in the middle of the dim room and gazed at her in speculation and pity, as she tried to climb the walls and the furniture and looked up at the windows I had shut as a precaution.

She came across and stared up at me, and nuzzled my bare feet with a cold wet nose. All my temptations to keep her as a pet vanished in compassion. I must try to return her to her family – it was the only fair thing. I thought too of the big dogs which Mr Brown would be bringing to the farmhouse, and of our unbadgerworthy bungalow now in building, through which she could tear her way in a few minutes: I thought of her loneliness, and how a free life with her own clan was so much better, even for a weaker member.

Back in bed I sat watching. She trundled on for a time round and round the room, passing under my bed at each circuit. I looked over the side and felt like someone in a boat watching fish. Finally she went back to her box and I to sleep.

In the morning I settled myself to write and keep an eye on her. Now I was determined to try to restore her to the wild, and tried to work out a plan that would be safe and certain for her. Goldie and I studied our photographs to see if we could identify her. The tiny cub was in several of these and looked very like her, right down to the scruffy sideways tail: it was probably she.

For most of that morning Arwen slept in a corner she had chosen for herself behind the chest of drawers. I covered her with towels, but presently I picked her up and put her back in the warm hay-box.

In the afternoon we went down to the Valley to try to establish for certain whether the family was at the main sett, and here we had a stroke of real luck. Bending to study the ground outside the tree-stump hole we suddenly heard a thudding of badgers' feet away from us down the tunnel. Probably near the exit because of warm weather they had suddenly awoken to hear our voices and had pounded away deeper. This was incredibly good fortune: now we *knew* that the badgers were at home. Time was very much a critical thing in our calculations. If the cub were returned before she was fully recovered she might collapse again, but the longer we kept her the greater the chance that her family would reject her. We thought that she was recovered enough now to be returned, but had not seen any way of avoiding keeping her for another night until we knew without doubt where her family was. In the ordinary way this would have meant another night's watching, but now that we knew the family was at home a whole twenty-four hours could be cut from our time-table.

Natalka I remember was worried about our whole project and wanted me to keep the cub. She thought that already it had been away too long for the family to receive it back, and that it would smell too much of human scent and probably be killed at once by members of the clan. As a trained zoologist Natalka is knowledgeable about animal behaviour, and I vacillated after she had telephoned. Finally Goldie and I decided to go on with our plan. From now on we touched the cub only with gloved hands. We made a thick lining of leafmould (gathered with gloves) inside the cat-basket, so that she should re-acquire a woodland odour. We debated and turned down the idea of making any identity mark, lest this should be one more thing to go against her reception; and then we gave her a last feed of bread-and-milk and put her into the basket.

Our plan was to release her a few feet from the lowest entrance of the main sett about half an hour before the badgers' usual emergence time. If she went down, as we hoped, she would have a little while to mingle with the other cubs and acquire some of their scent and to readjust herself before setting out with the family again for the night's foraging. It would also give us time to go back to the house for long-range photographic equipment and get with it to the ledges to see and photograph what happened.

We were half-way down the hill to the Valley gate when Natalka came running after us: concerned lest we were doing the wrong thing she had rushed out as soon as Nicholas returned with the car. There was a brief consultation at the gate and we said we were decided now to go on with the cub's return to the wild. I said that I thought freedom, to a wild animal, was everything, with all its risks and hazards. Natalka saw that we would not be deflected and came with us through the woods to the place we had decided on. The cub was scuffling in the basket – could she have scented or sensed her home country?

It was 7.30 p.m. when we came near the lower entrance to the main sett. Goldie put down the basket on the badgers' own path about ten feet from the entrance and opened the lid. The cub looked out, wrinkling her muzzle at the woodland air, then with a sudden eager leap was out, hurrying along the path to disappear unhesitatingly down into the hole.

We waited for a while before turning for home, lest we had been wrong and would see her again, fleeing for her life, but all was silence.

# CHAPTER TWENTY-ONE

THE family was late emerging, as we sat tense with anticipation on the ledges. It was nearly 9 p.m. when the whole clan came out complete with all five cubs among whom we easily recognized our tiny one, obviously delighted to be back. We very seldom see badgers go down to the stream, but she at once hustled down there to drink with another cub (chlorinated water in the farmhouse not acceptable ?), and then back up to the ramps again where she made the eager rounds like a child just home from boarding school – playing on all the branches where she had played before, licking our honey offerings in all the usual places and joyfully rootling for our raisins.

The adults and the other cubs nosed her, as if aware of some difference in scent, but clearly accepting her, and in the case of the sow whom we took to be the mother, grooming and guarding her in a most touching manner. We left while all were still playing or sitting in groups grooming themselves and each other, and the evening star was shining (for Arwen ?). Our Operation Evenstar had been wholly successful.

All three of us were delighted, but I was tired, in the blissful way one is at the successful end of a delicate and difficult enterprise. The roe buck leaping through the tall grass of Lower Naps put a seal on our pleasure as we walked home under wild roses and moons of elderflower.

The house seemed quiet without a badger-cub. It was strange to sleep undisturbed again, even after only a night of her company. In the morning I was out early, walking the rounds of the setts on both farms, but there was no sign of the cub. I trusted that she was safe now below ground with her family, as a wild cub should be: better dead than captive.

Goldie and I mucked out the hay and peat from my bedroom and made our plans for Arwen's full recovery and safety. She was so small, perhaps it was difficult for her in competition with the big ones to get enough food for proper growth and development. We thought of our success in feeding the Outlier fox-cubs, and of Arwen's readiness to take what we offered in the farmhouse.

The only way we could feed her now, we decided, was by feeding all the five cubs together. In no other way could we be certain that this small cub got her rights. That evening we took along to the main sett a small chicken-trough full of bread-and-milk and beaten egg with honey, and left it on a leafy platform between the lower and north holes, where the cubs often played.

Towards sunset with two friends, Pat and Aileen, we went along the stream to the ledges. At 8.45 in good daylight the family emerged from the north hole with all the cubs, and immediately detected the presence of something strange and interesting on the platform below them. The big boar (who had killed the vixen) went down and made several cautious approaches before finally sampling our offering and then returning to the watching family. The biggest cub, Bully Boy, next went down and dared the unknown, feeding at the trough for some minutes. Arwen, to our delight, was the next to risk it – she knew bread-and-milk – but after the first sniff she dashed back to the family on the ramp. Goldie whispered in my ear that perhaps it reminded her of captivity. But after a few minutes our cub returned and fed well and confidently.

It was a soft damp evening after the long drought. There was much coming and going of badgers in the summer rain that soaked into the parched earth. Never had we seen badgers go down to the stream so often. There was a rainy smell in the woods that somehow reminded us of malt – the effect of rain on something, but what?

The badgers dispersed at 9.20, and we also. We were to see a strange and wonderful thing.

Walking back along the Valley path we heard an urgent yikkering in the high woods across the stream and stood still to look and listen. A badger sow came running through the woods above us with two cubs, one of which was Arwen; the tiny cub was a little behind and she was the chattering one. The sow led the cubs right down to the stream-bank, three yards from where we stood on the further bank: it was almost as if she had brought our little one down to show us. We stood in some wonder, still and breathless. All three of the badgers knew that we were there and saw us. Then the sow turned and padded back with the cubs up the bank, through the trees and ferns. Arwen was yikkering loudly behind her as if crying, 'Don't leave me behind again! It's too steep!'

The sow turned to help her, grasping her scruff and gently hauling her upwards; and more astonishing still but clearly seen by all of us, the bigger cub pushed with his shoulder from behind. We four on the path watched scarcely believing as the badgers disappeared slowly in the woods. It was a great day.

Goldie and I kept up a regular meals-in-trough service, nightly watching Arwen and the other cubs making full use of it. Quite soon, after Bully Boy had attempted to take the trough underground, we were compelled to tether it to a low tree-branch, hiding the string under leaf-mould which the cubs soon scattered.

Arwen began to show characteristics which we were later often to see. She was easily the most enterprising, intelligent and courageous of the cubs. After the first night or two she began to come out well before the others, scurrying down to the trough to get her rations in peace without the jostling of the gang.

'I'm afraid we must admit that our cub has quite the worst tail,' Goldie said, 'but far the best I.Q. of all of them.'

Still I made my careful early morning rounds, anxious lest disaster should again have overtaken the cub, but all was well. I remember my pleasure in the summer flowering grasses silvered with dew, tall and very beautiful, the foxgloves like banners above them. Bill was haymaking again (the long Brown delays continuing; something had to be done about the grass) and hay was in most of the fields, lying in patterned swaths or baled or windrowed; a heavenly smell drifted over the whole farm.

We were towards the middle of June when our solicitors prevailed on us to set a deadline for Mr Brown. This was to be June 30, the farm to be placed on the market again if contracts were not exchanged by that date. I was about to leave for Malta with Natalka and Nicholas, who were attending a seabed conference there, and I left without news from Mr Brown but hoping for a settlement in my absence.

Mr Brown did not meet the deadline, I learned with disappointment on my return. The farm was re-offered, but this time reserving the Orchard plot and the whole of the Wild Valley. Now began again the trail of prospective buyers and now again Goldie protected me from their invasions; until quite quickly someone who seemed of our own kind came and said that she wanted the old farm, and proceedings began immediately.

Suddenly the truth really came home to me: we were not to lose the Wild Valley! After all my grief for its loss it was back in our keeping – and as far as I can see, for always. Never would I dream of letting it go again – *I fling them back their gold—;* never before had I dreamed of its value to me.

Goldie and I saw in a flash that our old policy of maintaining our distance from the badgers, for the sake of their survival, need no longer be continued. No one but ourselves would have power over them, and the power we had would never be used except in their favour.

We began with subdued excitement to resume watches on the near side of the stream and close to the main sett. Instead of leaving our raisins in places to be viewed from the ledges we scattered them on the grassy track to Valley field, and made sitting places among the trees there.

The best thing of all in our watching of these badgers was about to begin, and this was our relation with Arwen, the cub we had returned to the wild.

All the badgers came up on to the track, quickly discovering the new place for their raisins and peanuts; the cubs came closer than the adults but Arwen came closest of all. On the first night, after foraging peacefully for some time a few feet away from us, she climbed on to a tree stump just across the track and sat down looking at us with interest. She did this for several nights, even when Rover was sitting with us (he of course taking all things for granted), and once when Haile was there and suddenly chased all the cubs away, to my horror, although I think he meant it in play. I thought after this that the cub would not come so close again and was careful to leave Haile behind; but she came even closer, on both sides of us and all around, so that she must have had strong whiffs of our scent. We began laying the nut and raisin trail right up to us, to see how close she would come. The other four stopped as usual about eight feet away but Arwen came up and snuffled out raisins from under the edge of our jeans, her muzzle tickling us.

With the standard lens Goldie began photographing this unusual happening, the wild cub coming out of the woods of her own free will to forage close to a human sitting there, and her success was immediate. The camera and Goldie were just across the track, at the tree stump where Arwen had first sat looking at us; we had one flash-gun on the camera and a second on a branch to one side. Arwen – and the other cubs at a small distance – took no notice, but the adults kept further away always, and often we did not see them on the track at all.

Every evening we would set out for our appointment, and every evening, as the sun went down and her star came up, Arwen would come trotting out of the trees towards us. Now I could hold in my hand a saucer of farm honey (she refused shop honey brought for her by Aileen!) and she would eat from it, placing a paw on the rim to steady it and licking my thumb indiscriminately, so that I wondered if one day she would eat it in mistake, so honeyed was it.

She was still much the smallest of the cubs but she was growing plump and bouncy. When other cubs came too near her own foraging she would swing her rump at them as cubs do, and once I heard her hiss, as a cat or cobra hisses. She was well able to look out for herself, we were pleased and relieved to notice, remembering the cold limp body she had been.

Her boldness and confidence seemed to increase nightly. Except for Bully Boy, who would come around our feet, the other cubs kept their distance; but Arwen ate from our bare hands the first time we tried it. Soon her front paws were planted on us and she was nosing into pockets. A raisin fallen under a gumboot was easy to reach by scraping away the boot. Torch and camera-flash did not disturb her at all, nor did our movements to replenish the raisins in the open hand.

It was still only September when Goldie and I were able to stroke her. She did not care much for a hand above her, but would calmly allow rubbing under her throat and round her muzzle; and we could tickle her sides to draw attention to fresh offerings in the hand. She was still truly wild, in that any unusual noise (sometimes not heard by us) would send her flying back to the sett, but she would return almost at once, hurrying back to us: and when all the food was finished, and a paw scraped on our chests produced no more, she would sit companionably beside us and belch a little and groom herself, as if we were all badgers together.

It may seem scarcely possible that this should happen to us twice, but six weeks after agreeing to buy the farm our second purchaser suddenly withdrew, for financial reasons.

Now, tired of private purchasers and their delays and shortcomings, we instructed our agents to offer the farm at auction, as we ourselves had bought it twenty-three years ago. And this is where my story of the Valley and the farm comes to its undecided end. Our new house is built – I can see it through the window as I write – but we cannot move into it. We live in the farmhouse, keeping it warm and cared for, but like people on sufferance, prepared to depart. Two years after the accident, we still do not know who will own the farm. Somehow it does not seem to matter so much now that we know who will, for the rest of a lifetime, own the Valley.